The Gift

Psychic Surgery in the Philippines

I0087217

Blood, Guts & Spiritual Healing

Secrets of the Psychic Surgeons

GAIL THACKRAY

Copyright © Dec 2015 Gail Thackray

All rights reserved. No part of this book may be reproduced or transmitted in any form or by any means, electronic or mechanical, including photocopying, recording, or by any information storage and retrieval system without written permission of the publisher, except for the inclusion of brief quotations in a review.

The author of this book does not dispense medical advice or prescribe the use of any technique as a form of treatment for physical or medical problems without the advice of a physician. The intent of the author is only to offer information of a general nature to help you in your quest for emotional or spiritual well-being. In the event you use any of the information in this book for yourself, which is your constitutional right, the author and the publisher assume no responsibility for your actions.

All opinions expressed herein are solely the author's. They do not represent the official positions of any organization, group, or business mentioned. Additionally, the events contained herein are described to the best of the author's knowledge and recollection. Any deviation from fact is unintentional and regretted, and neither the author nor the publisher can be held responsible for any errors contained herein.

Some of the names of the people mentioned in this book have been changed.

CONTENTS

CHAPTER 1

Blood, Guts, and Spiritual Healing

I had heard about the famed Filipino "psychic surgeons" who put their patients into a kind of spiritual trance and then perform actual surgeries on them. And I mean with blood, guts, and everything! They supposedly open up the body without instruments, place their hands inside, and even pull out tumors and things—all without anesthetic! How? It is done in the name of spiritual healing, with lots of prayer and faith. Could this actually be real?

My dear pal Robert had been to the Philippines and had met one of these amazing healers. He told me incredible stories, and I knew I just had to see this for myself. For some time we had talked about going to meet his friend, a psychic surgeon named Ambrosio. Robert said that he'd seen Ambrosio do real surgeries using only his bare hands. He'd cut the person open and then place his fingers inside! Robert, himself, had even had a psychic surgery. What went through my head was: "You're kidding me! This stuff is real?" With a fascination for the paranormal, I had come across many extraordinary things, but this I had to see.

Robert and I had become close friends during my many trips to Abadiania, home of the Brazilian healer, John of God. At age forty I had experienced a life-changing epiphany, becoming a medium and suddenly doing freaky things myself. I awakened an ability to talk to spirits on the other side, and I had fallen into my life path as a psychic and spiritual healer. A few years later I took a trip to Brazil to explore the healing work of John of God. John of God goes into a trance, incorporates spirits inside his body, and then performs miraculous healings. I had simply gone out of curiosity and was blown away.

While there, I'd received downloads from spirit which raised my own healing and psychic abilities considerably. I loved being at John of God's healing center so much that I started taking groups of clients to Brazil. This is where Robert and I met. Robert was the first person to bring groups to the healing center, and he had spent many years with John of God. Robert and I share a deep love for the work of John of God. We also share an interest in any real spiritual healing.

Most of the work that John of God does involves performing an "invisible surgery," also known as a "spiritual intervention," which changes a person's energy field and often results in healing them, not just physically, but also emotionally and spiritually. Although the majority of healings performed by John of God are invisible surgeries, a small percentage involve an actual physical surgery. This is what normally gets the most attention, as he actually cuts people open without anesthetic. He says that this method of healing is not any stronger than an invisible surgery, but sometimes people need to see a physical action happening, something so amazing to the eye, to be able to believe in the healing.

John of God will take a few volunteers on stage and do actual physical surgeries on them. He will cut open their flesh with a sharp knife, perhaps remove something, and then sew the incision closed, just like a real surgery! Other times he will place a massive forceps into the person's nose or scrape their eye with a kitchen knife—all without anesthetic and no apparent pain to the patient! This is completely impossible to our western way of thinking. However, having seen this now hundreds of times, I know for certain that it is possible, it does happen, and it is completely real!

Having experienced John of God and seen other amazing healers, I did believe in spiritual healing. Still, powerful healers like John of God are very rare indeed. The Filipino healers have a different style where they open up a person and make an incision without actually cutting them with a knife. Robert had met the psychic healer, Ambrosio, years earlier in the Philippines while on a trip with his now ex-wife, Katarina.

Being a medium and energy healer myself, I was intrigued to learn more. I felt like a child in training next to the likes of John of God, whose healing center was a place that I had learned and grown substantially. What else did the world have to offer? You are always learning and developing, and I wanted to see what I could learn from the healers of the Philippines. Plus, I believe that part of my journey is to share this psychic world with everyone, and I knew that many people back home would love to hear all about it.

Robert told me about his first meeting with Ambrosio about 15 years ago. He and his wife, Katarina, had traveled to Baguio in the Philippines. A jeweler by trade, Robert would go several times a year to purchase quality silver. This particular trip was to stand out as a very unusual one. Katarina, who was also an energy healer, had heard about the Filipino psychic surgeons and wanted to experience going to one. So Robert brought his wife on the trip with the intention of finding a psychic surgeon. As Robert recalls his trip, he describes his ex-wife as an amazingly talented spiritual healer with a tremendous connection to spirit. "Her connection to the real world however left much to be desired," Robert groaned.

When they arrived at the hotel Robert had booked, Katarina said, "No, this is not the right one." Katarina was very particular that she wanted to stay at a specific hotel that was not the one Robert had booked. Robert rolled his eyes, as he was used to this strange behavior. She did everything by "knowing," by gut feeling, which could sometimes drive Robert crazy. Arriving at the "right" hotel, she inquired about spiritual healers in the area. The receptionist couldn't find the card that he wanted, but then it miraculously appeared on the counter. On it was the number for the psychic healer, Ambrosio. It so happened that Ambrosio was practicing in his "clinic" only a few steps from their hotel.

The next day, when Robert and Katarina arrived at the clinic, Ambrosio was already waiting for them; he knew they were coming. Robert described the clinic as what looked to be a beaten up, old metal garage complete with a roll-up door. Inside it was simple, a makeshift bench as a healing table and couple of chairs. As he opened his morning clinic, people gathered and lined up along the street.

Ambrosio began the healing session holding the Holy Bible and reciting prayers until such time as the energy was strong enough for him to begin. Then, one by one, each person was guided to lie on his work table. He started by running his hands over them, pressing down and holding the energy on certain areas. The patient was prepped for surgery by having their clothing pulled back by a layer of cotton wool, leaving an exposed abdomen or chest.

Then the psychic surgery began. Robert said that Ambrosio would place his two index fingers together on the patient's bare skin. Then, as he pulled his fingers apart, a thin cut would form on their body. A small amount of blood would gather at the site, and Ambrosio slipped his fingers deeper into the flesh. Then, when the healing was complete, he would wave his hand and the wound would be closed, leaving only a thin red mark where the surgery had occurred. As Robert described the scene, I thought, *Oh Wow! This sounds crazy. I have to see this for myself!*

Of course Robert and Katarina were impressed by the healings, and they decided to stay longer in Baguio. In fact, they were glued to Ambrosio and attended the clinic every day for two weeks. Each and every day, they continued to be amazed.

Robert described how, as he left the clinic the first day and actually every day thereafter, the energy was so strong that he could barely walk. A loud buzzing, like high-powered electric lines running through his head, persisted for hours. He said his whole body felt like a surge of electricity had passed through it. He was energized and vibrating, yet he was physically tired and his bones ached. It was as if he had been beaten with a hammer "but in a good way." He could do nothing but collapse into bed and sleep until the next day.

During the two weeks, they saw miraculous things. They both received healings. Most of the healing was energetic, but Ambrosio also performed "psychic surgeries" where he actually opened their body. Robert said it didn't hurt. Afterwards the "incision" was closed, but he could see the faint red line for days, evidence of the psychic surgery.

Then one day, Ambrosio said he would open their chakras. He took Robert's hands and proceeded to open the chakras in his palms. As Ambrosio pressed into the center of each palm and asked the chakra to open, a small drop of blood appeared. Robert said that the opening of the chakras in his hands was an amazing experience and that he felt much more energy running through his body. Though afterwards, he was inexplicably tired.

Towards the end of their stay, Katarina and Robert were allowed to place their hands in someone's body to see what it felt like. With Ambrosio's fingers guiding him, Robert noted that the body seemed to open easily. Katarina said that it felt like "warm butter." Hearing this made me yearn to have this incredible experience as well.

It had been years since they had been in touch, but Robert said he would try to arrange a visit. Since their last contact was before the Internet became ubiquitous, finding him might prove difficult. Miraculously, Robert was able to track him down immediately. Ambrosio was thrilled about us coming, and it almost seemed like he was expecting us.

Divine timing set this in motion. It just so happened that I was going to be on that side of the world, speaking in Perth, Australia, and Robert had a wedding to attend in Bali. Bali seemed like a wonderful place for Robert and me to meet. From there we could easily fly to the Philippines, and the promise of an exciting journey was set into play. I knew that this trip would be profound, but I really had no idea what I was in for.

CHAPTER 2

Bali, the Island of Dreams

We had a quick five or six days in Bali, and I was determined to see as much as I could squeeze in before going to the Philippines. I had looked up "spiritual places" on the Internet and found a slew of Hindu temples, magnificent places of worship, and a wonderful array of spiritual sites to visit. Of course there was also the beautiful, lush tropical terrain of Bali, with mountains, waterfalls, and stunning beaches.

What I really couldn't imagine until I arrived was the massive amount of incredible culture everywhere. I envisioned having to drive far from the main cities in order to see a few sacred places. Yet every street was lined with beautiful hand-carved statues. Every corner revealed an amazing display of artwork, a tremendous statue, or an ornate building. There were temples everywhere! Ornate displays of offerings to the spirits were also widespread, but not just outside the temples—everywhere. Every house, every business, every building with a statue, all were displaying an offering to the spirits.

Robert remarked that there wasn't a scrap of graffiti to be found; creative expression was found in different ways. All around us, everything was an expression of art. The culture here stimulated beautiful, imaginative creations—an outlet for every artist's dream.

There was so much to see that we needed a personal tour guide. God sent us the perfect guide, Marti, who would also be our driver for the week. So off we went to explore. We visited beautiful temples far and wide, in the mountains and near the water. We bowed to the centuries-old sacred statues. We rode elephants through the river. We saw butterflies emerging from their cocoons. We visited healing waters into which you could dip your feet and say a prayer. Praying seemed to be of prime importance. Making offerings to the gods was an extensive pastime. Unlike those of us back home who might light a candle, say a quick prayer and we're done, they spent hours making careful platters of fruit and plants to sacrifice to the afterworld.

Robert made a great travel companion. We are clearly old soul mates with a special bond, both with an urge for adventure and a good sense of humor. Part of my reason for coming was to film my experiences for my documentaries. Robert got to hold the camera and document my every move. He wanted to be called Cecil from now on after Cecil B. DeMille, the great movie director/producer who made the film *The Ten Commandments*. This was very funny because when Robert made this request, he didn't realize the significance of his joke. My home in Los Angeles was once owned by Mr. DeMille, and I often feel that his spirit is around.

How can one go to Bali without visiting the palm reader and medicine man, Ketut Liyer? Ketut was made famous by the book *Eat Pray Love* and subsequent film starring Julie Roberts. Yes, he is a real person. *Eat Pray Love* put Ketut, and indeed Bali, on the spiritual tour map.

I'd heard mixed reviews about Ketut from those who have visited him. Some were less than impressed with their readings, which took only a few minutes and said general things like: "You will marry, have children, and divorce." Still, I was very excited to sit with this famous man of wisdom.

Ketut is actually the name given to any second born son in Bali, so there are actually thousands of them! But this particular Ketut is the one and only from the film. Since the book and film were released, Ketut has become the face of healing in Bali, and his time consumed with tourists from all over the world. To get to Ketut one has to take the journey to Ubud. Ubud is a small, artsy town about an hour and a half from the airport and many of the popular beach resorts. The drive was stunning. We passed copious amounts of fine architecture, culture, and, in particular, stone statues of various gods lining nearly every highway, street, and small town we crossed.

We were told that Ketut is not always able to see people. At 95 years old, his health has good days and bad days. We prayed for a good day, and we were rewarded with a particularly spritely and happy healer. With one tooth in his head and a sun-beaten face, he looks like he's over a hundred. I surmise that he actually has lost track of his age, so 95 might be a guess. Though clearly his is a face of wisdom.

The sign outside let us know that we were entering his place of healing, which was also his personal home. It was a sprawling set up: a courtyard filled with several buildings and, of course, statues and offerings throughout. There even appeared to be a central "home temple" inside.

I was surprised that I recognized the center from the film. Clearly they had authentically shot everything just the way he had been living and working for many years. In fact, he was seated waiting for us on the veranda, just as he had been in the film.

His energy was beautiful. He smiled big, hearty, real, loving smiles and laughed. He started by reading my face lines (plenty of those to read), then the lines in my palms. He said, "The lines of great influence and success," a theme that appeared to show up on several areas of my body and even my ears. Who knew! I hoped that he was correct.

Ketut's son was there to help if any translation was needed. Although Ketut was difficult to understand, his broken English was good enough, and his body language said the rest. He presumed the cameraman, Robert, was my husband and continued to make jokes about how he thought that I must have a lot of energy for my husband. In fact, he said it was in my lines! I think he was just being fun and probably says that to all middle-aged women, who like me, probably blush and smile. He said that he was too old and ugly for me and only had one tooth. True, he lacked teeth, but his face was a beautiful one, full of joy and wisdom.

He asked me to turn as he "read" my back and neck. At this point I felt warm chills down my spine. I knew he was really doing healing work. Of course! He is called a medicine man. I wondered if the "reading" was just light chitchat while he really did a deeper subconscious energy healing for whatever the person actually needs. Anyway, that was my take on it.

I left in bliss, feeling way more energized and floaty than a normal palm reading would give. I wanted to share this energy, this feeling. So with this intention, I went in search of prayer beads that I might bring home. I found them at a market close to the Elephant Cave Temple and healing waters. I was told the prayer beads were the "real deal," ones made from fruit seeds. They cost a little more than the plain wood beads, but they were well worth it.

Afterward, I decided to return to Ketut. He seemed to know that I would be returning. I asked him if I could have a special blessing for my prayer beads, which I was wearing. He asked me to remove them. He and his son examined them closely, running their fingers over them. "You know, these are sacred prayer beads that we use when we pray to the gods," he told me. I nodded. He added, "These are very nice, real ones."

Ketut took the prayer beads in his hands and asked what I wanted them for. I told him, "For my people at home that could not come and for good health and prosperity." He smiled and began a mantra. The mantra lasted a minute or two and had the most beautiful energy. (My guide later told me that he was speaking in Sanskrit.) He placed the blessed beads over my head, and the energy sent chills down my spine.

All in all, the visit with Ketut was a once in a lifetime, beautiful experience–one I would not have missed for the world.

CHAPTER 3

Cakoda and the Mysterious Healing

Our driver, Marti, now knowing the types of things we were interested in, said that he, too, knew a local healer and could introduce us. Of course my reaction was, "Wow, absolutely!" So the next day, off we went on another adventure to meet the healer Cakoda.

I don't think Cakoda is well known to foreigners, but he seems to be quite popular with the locals. He came highly recommended from Marti, who had heard about his healings through the grapevine. The fame of Ketut seems to have also brought people to Bali who are interested in seeking out other healers and soothsayers as well.

We arrive at the residence and healing center of Cakoda. Like Ketut's place, and many other beautiful Bali residences, they are not designed as a typical house in the US. They are more like sprawling complexes with several buildings for different family members, all within a walled garden. Each of the bedrooms may be a separate, small building. Even the kitchen may be its own stand-alone building. Usually there is also a small temple or altar and several statues of the Hindu gods. Cakoda's place was beautiful with lovely, ornate buildings and lots of outdoor living space and verandas. There were also what appeared to be gravesites or memorials.

As we wandered through the beautiful, tranquil grounds, we came across a small gathering on a raised patio. A group of about ten people sat cross-legged in a semi-circle, their attention focused on a person who was clearly a healer. He was a beautiful, thin man with shoulder-length grey hair. He wore a simple white robe and his feet were bare. Even though he was older, he appeared to be high energy and in good health. His energy passed over the group, soothing and loving.

We noticed that he was working on a client. First he checked several points on her head, seeming to touch meridian lines and pressure points. From these points, and perhaps using psychic insight, he told her about an issue that she had and what vitamins to take. Then he asked her to lie down on a mat. He took what looked like a black lacquer chopstick and ran it gently over her body, as if marking lines over her energy body. Then he used the "chopstick" on her toes.

A volunteer ushered me to sit with the group. It appeared the healer was taking clients, one at a time, as they arrived, and we were told to sit and observe until our time. There was a steady stream of new comers, always about ten people waiting. I saw that some placed money in a donation box. The typical amount appeared to be the equivalent of about $20. I was told that the money went to his chosen charity, a local children's school (as well as some money for him to live off).

Two small Shih Tzu dogs wandered up from the garden. They checked me out, walked over me, and made a beeline to sit under Cakoda's chair. Clearly they were helping with the healing sessions.

It was my turn, and I went to greet this beautiful healer. He was sitting in his chair and motioned me to sit on the floor in front of him with my back turned to him. He started to press certain pressure points on my head, neck, and face. He felt the groove behind my ears and checked my throat. As he did so, he made comments like, "Yes, that is fine…a little bit there…this should be ok…oh, here…yes, here is an issue." He pressed on a point on the top of my skull, and I almost leapt off the floor. Yes, he had found a "spot," whatever that meant!

His English was good. Even with a strong accent there was no need for a translator.

"What can I do for you?" he asked.

I told him that I was pretty healthy, but a little help with my eye would be nice.

"That's that point here," he said, as he pushed the same point on my skull.

"Ouch!" I exclaimed.

"This is where the block is," he noted.

He motioned for me to lie down and he touched points on my face. Using the chopstick, he seemed to run meridian lines and stop gently at certain pressure points on my body. Robert said that he has seen some of this work in a type of hypnosis, so maybe I was being relaxed and worked on. Then he took the end of the chopstick and firmly pressed it into deliberate spots on my toes.

Toe by toe, he tested them. "This should be good…this

should be fine...now this one is going to hurt a bit...," he forewarned me. He was correct again as I nearly leapt off the mat. He drew some imaginary lines over my body with his stick as if to do a psychic surgery. When he used the chopstick to retest the exact same spot on my toe, miraculously it was now much more bearable. I was certainly convinced that some kind of block had been removed.

He then sat back in his chair with me sitting in front of him once again. He instructed me to open my jaw wide. He then placed one of his fingers in each of my ears. I felt my ears open up and his finger slid all the way down under my jawbone and inside my mouth. He now asked me to close my jaw. I did so and my jawbone snapped over his finger and something clearly popped. , I thought. He repeated it again two or three times until it appeared completely adjusted.

I told him that I'd brought the names of many people from back home, as well as the many viewers would be watching what we were filming, all who would love to receive some of this beautiful energy. I asked him if he could bless the prayer beads and volcanic stones I'd brought. He smiled and then climbed up to reach a glass bottle of oil that was on a high shelf. He asked me to hold the objects in my hand as he carefully placed a drop of oil on each one and then rubbed it with intent. It smelled like Frankincense, but I didn't ask; he looked focused. I was honored that Cakoda spent a lot of time with me. I thanked him and wished him many blessings. .

I stayed for a few minutes to talk to others that were still in the waiting area. Most of them appeared to have only minor ailments and were there for more of a "spiritual checkup." Nobody had anything too serious. It was obvious that several had visited before. When I asked them about Cakoda, I was told stories about their friends who had been cured of cancer or received other miraculous healings. All spoke about his gentle soul, loving energy, and passion for his charitable cause, the children's school. He seemed adored by all.

Later, back in my hotel, I thought about the move he had done with his fingers in my ears. The strange thing was that when I tried to do it to myself, there was no way I could get a finger in that far. None of my fingers were thin enough to go in that far! Besides there was also an eardrum in the way! Yet his finger had easily slid all the way through. I couldn't figure it out. It was impossible, but I knew he had done it. I'd felt it; it was very real. For days I kept trying to do it; I even tried using a Q-tip. There was simply no way it could be done! The more and more I thought about it, I realized that something really wonderful and mysterious had happened that day.

It wasn't until a week or so later that I checked out the video footage. As it came to the part where he stuck his fingers in my ears, I slowed down the video to watch intently. Which fingers did he actually use? To my surprise—none! I couldn't believe it. I had quite clearly and definitely felt him put his fingers through my ears. I had felt my jawbone rolling over his fingers. Yet on the video footage, all his fingers are visible and covering my ears the entire time! Now I was certain he had done something supernatural and miraculous. He couldn't have been trying to trick me because he'd never even said what he was going to do. He never told me that he was going to put his finger in my ear nor did he give me the expectation that I'd feel something. He just did his healing work without saying a word. Cleary that was some very powerful healing.

What exactly he was healing, I wasn't sure. But then I realized that when I was in sitting in the waiting area, I had been wishing that my daughter was with me. My daughter has quite a severe jaw or TMJ issue, but she was back home in California. While I sat there, I wondered if he could do a distance healing on her. *Probably better to bring her in person though because she wasn't very open to believing in this type of thing.* Perhaps Cakoda had heard me telepathically and was actually working on her. When I got home a few weeks later, I inquired about her jaw.

"Actually, it's not been bothering me as much recently," she remarked.

"That's good," I simply said and smiled to myself. I wasn't about to spoil it by sharing anything that she might think is weird, and having her somehow bring the problem back to prove mom wrong.

I was a little sorry to leave Bali. There was so much to see and definitely not enough time. But now for our adventure in the Philippines!

CHAPTER 4

Anthony, Touched by an Angel

To get to Baguio, the home of Ambrosio, you have to fly into Manila. You then usually need to stay overnight to catch a bus in the morning. We arrived in Manila about 3 p.m. and had the evening to ourselves before our Baguio bus in the morning. Most normal people would have had a nice relaxing evening. Robert even suggested we catch a lounge show at one of the big hotels. Hell no! I was already on the Internet seeing if there was anything of spiritual significance in the area that we might be able to film.

Lo and behold, I came across a psychic healer, Anthony Vivero. His name seemed to jump off the page. He was in the area and from looking at his photo, I could tell his energy was beautiful. I wanted to meet him. Still, what was the chance of meeting him this very evening? Searching a little deeper, I found out that he held group clinics where all are welcome but only on Wednesdays and Saturdays from 11 a.m. to 7 p.m. OMG it was Saturday at 3 p.m.! It was meant to be!

We hired a taxi and an hour later, after getting a bit lost, we arrived at the home of Anthony Vivero. It was in a residential neighborhood, but as we came around the corner, there was no mistaking this was the place. There was an altar and about fifty chairs set up on a patio. A number of people were gathered and it was clear that the man who was leading the group was Anthony.

They welcomed us as first-timers. We explained who we were and that we would love to observe and, if possible, film. Anthony was more than accommodating, inviting me up on his "stage" to sit by him through the whole evening. He also shared for us on camera, each and every healing. *Wow!* This was a two-hour, up close and personal interview with the healer himself in action.

What struck me immediately was that he continued having conversations, talked to me, offered us coffee and snacks, joked and conversed, all while doing healing work. How could he do this? Wasn't it disturbing his concentration? Apparently not. He said that he multitasks in life and doesn't need any kind of concentration to do the healing.

His story is that he was a regular businessman (in his words not a particular good man, certainly not a holy man) when one night a spirit came to visit him. He said that it was a powerful, awesome vision and definitely not a dream. It was unlike anything he had ever experienced. He said that the spirit told him he would be a healer and gave him instructions. The spirit gave him a sort of "energy gift" and explained how he would place his hands on people. Anthony said that it was an intense night; he was shaking, scared, overwhelmed, and emotional. It went on all night long! Still, he didn't believe it. He didn't think others would believe him. How would he even start healing? Why would people even come to him? Anthony was told not to worry, that he would be given the information to make people believe.

A week later another spirit came and told him about a famous Filipino actress who would go to Peru and Africa and needed to be warned of some grave danger. If the actress were to go, she would surely be killed there, the spirit told him. He wrote notes on a pad by his bedside. After he woke up, he was able to get this message to the actress. She was stunned. Anthony had details about the trip no one knew but her. As a result, she didn't take the trip, and it was all over the news. Overnight, Anthony was famous. People flocked from all over to see him. Thus his healing clinic was started and people lined up to be healed by him.

Anthony actually paused the session for a few minutes while he told the story in multiple languages so that everyone could understand, and then even played us the news clip. He also showed us the original note he had scribbled. It was now in a binder along with numerous other press clippings he'd received since. That was 16 years ago. He still works as a businessman and hosts clinics twice a week where he heals people. This is his real passion.

What was so endearing about him was that not only does he clearly care about the people he treats, but he also refuses all donations. He says that he makes plenty from his businesses and never accepts anything for the healing. He even returned a donation from an Arab prince for $20,000, saying he simply couldn't accept it. I thought this man was a true saint.

I call him a healer and not a psychic surgeon because he heals through the "laying of the hands" and using anointing oil. He does not open the body like other Filipino healers. When we visited, as each client came up, he placed a small swab of anointing oil on their wrist. He then held their wrist and was connecting to their pulse. He appeared to tune into their energy as they chatted in a causal relaxed way. He explained that as he held their pulse, he was given information from spirit about their entire body. Then he would place his hands wherever they were needed, and perhaps asking the person to stand or turn. He seemed to be directing healing energy to the areas needed.

Several clients spoke to me. One had become paralyzed years before and, after only one session, had got up and walked away. Another had been cured of HIV three months prior and showed me the medical test results from before and after the healing–positive before and completely clear after.

He saved me until last. "Ok, let's take a look at you," he said placing a small amount of oil on my wrist and holding his fingers over my pulse. Anthony scanned my energy body psychically. He said that I had minor problems with my lower back and kidney (true). He placed an anointing oil in these places. Then he spent a few seconds placing his hands over these areas and directing energy. The energy from his hands felt warm, beautiful, and soothing.

I asked Anthony about my people at home. I am sure they were receiving the energy. He said that some people feel it and receive it. He believes that to come in person is a show of faith of the desire to be healed and therefore it is stronger. Still, if people can't come, he heals at a distance. Some of the "patients" there had brought pictures of loved ones. They also asked for blessings for their new business, if an ad for their new business was good, and even if they could locate a lost cell phone.

I was convinced Anthony has a special gift. He does what seems to be termed in these parts a "Magnetic Healing."

CHAPTER 5

The Long Haul
to Baguio

Baguio is a small town high in the mountain region of the northern Philippines. It has become famous as the home of the spiritual healers or psychic surgeons. Some say it is the energy of the mountains themselves that brings enlightenment and carries "The Gift" of psychic surgery.

There used to be flights to Baguio but that was a hair-raising, dangerous proposition. After several accidents they decided to close it to commercial flights, leaving only one way to get there, the long slow haul by bus. Actually, the last commercial flight to Baguio had the president's son on board. Apparently a Filipino psychic predicted a plane crash and got word to the President. The airplane was turned around and the President's son disembarked. I suppose no one informed the other passengers or they were not as superstitious and the plane continued. It did indeed crash into the mountains in Baguio. True Story!

Anyway, a bus was now the only option. The "Victory Line," Robert explained, was the way to go. It offers first class tickets on a super express coach with air conditioning and a "comfort room" (bathroom). The other "regular" option is to grab your chickens and hang on! During all the commotion at the bus depot, we somehow got ushered onto the wrong bus. Actually, I guess the regular one has been upgraded since Robert was last there as I didn't see any chickens on board. It was a 7-hour ride through the little villages, which I didn't mind so much, compared to the 6-hour express. In and out of a semi-sleep state I got to experience the countryside of the Philippines. Once in a while we'd get to stop and eat snacks among the locals. I think that we were the only white folks on the bus, and the other passengers were very entertained by us filming everything. Robert had to tell the bus driver that I was once on *Bay Watch* and that was it, the whole busload was informed.

Filipinos seem to love anything Americana. Robert filled me in that the Americans came to the Philippines and took over in the early 1900s. Before that they were under a repressive Spanish rule, but the Americans kicked out the Spaniards and were much nicer to the Filipinos. This explains the Jeepneys, which are a popular taxi-bus hybrid that look like an American army jeep, stretched back to fill a busload of people. All are vividly decorated with American-style graphics. I chuckled to myself at the very American sign on the side of ours, "How am I driving 1-800…?" It also explains their love for processed food and Spam, of all things! This was all great because we were instantly liked and most of the people on the bus could speak at least understandable English. The long bus ride gave us a good taste of the country and the culture. For about ten dollars, you couldn't beat the tour.

Manila is a densely populated city, with urban issues such as pollution, traffic, and over-crowding. It is actually the most densely populated city in the world right now. As the bus drove toward Baguio and started to climb the mountains, the lush green hills gave a natural beauty to the area, and the air was decidedly more fresh and clear than in Manila. This is, after all, a place where Filipinos vacation, particularly for the air quality.

Finally arriving in Baguio, we were met by the great healer himself, Ambrosio. We asked if he had been waiting at the bus station long; we hadn't even told him which bus we were on.

"Oh, about 10 minutes, that's all."

I suppose that is a perk of being psychic.

I immediately fell in love with Ambrosio, in a spiritual way of course. It was like I had known him for lifetimes, and we were finally reconnecting. He gave me a big warm hug and a glow of beautiful warm energy surrounded us. It had been 15 years since Robert had last laid eyes on him, but you could tell the fondness between them had never waned. As we left for a taxi, I noticed that Ambrosio walked with a limp. When he found an appropriate moment, Robert took me aside and shared, "I think he's had a stroke or something. I can't believe he never told me." Ambrosio ended up telling us the whole story over dinner.

First we checked into the hotel. I was nicely surprised. It was a little cabin-style complex, "The John Hay Camp," set on a mountaintop among beautiful pine forests. It reminded me of cabins in the national forest in northern California. It turned out that it was an American settlement founded in 1912. I had chosen it on the Internet, wanting to avoid a commercial-looking hotel that would be noisy. I'd come across a quaint cabin in a beautiful setting that would be lovely for meditation and spiritual work. I had gotten perfectly lucky or, of course, spiritually-guided.

We found an equally quaint restaurant with an outside patio among the pines. It was here that Ambrosio shared his story. He had received "The Gift" from his mother, who had in return had received it from her mother. As a young boy, Ambrosio used to assist his mother, who was the local village healer. Spiritual healing was not only believed, but it was considered quite normal in these parts. In fact, it was really the only option, as most had neither the money nor the ability to travel to see a medical doctor. So all the people here in the mountains relied on spiritual healers. Ambrosio's mother use to "lay the hands" and do "magnetic healing," which I came to understand was a type of energy healing similar to Reiki. She did not do "Psychic Surgery," which was the sensational type of healing that Ambrosio had become famous for. This is the style of healing where the healer actually enters the body, putting fingers or even whole hands inside. This, of course, includes blood guts and other impressive indications of physical surgery.

Ambrosio remembers watching his grandmother work when he was very young. She did psychic surgery, opening the body to heal. Then, when his Mother became the healer for the area, Ambrosio was by her side. He watched and assisted, learning how to take care of people. Then, in his twenties, his mother was ready to step down and it was Ambrosio's time to become the healer for the area. Ambrosio was not convinced he could do it, but his mother assured him that he could.

Then it was time, and his mother passed Ambrosio "The Gift." Though Ambrosio's mother had sought out another healer to give Ambrosio the actual initiation. This healer, Placito, opened Ambrosio's chakras and indoctrinated him as an official spiritual healer. Still, upon his mother's death, Ambrosio didn't believe he had the gift of healing to be able to continue his mother's work. He didn't have the confidence or belief in himself. But the town's people disagreed. Who else was to do it? His mother had been the only one in the area and now, "The Gift" had been passed to her son. They came to Ambrosio. They didn't question it, they just expected him to heal them, and thus it started.

Ambrosio not only continued his mother's work but also became well known in the region. He would have a practice where people came from all over to visit him and get a session at his clinic. Later he would take his healing work all over the world. His work included magnetic healing, as his mother had done, but more people sought him out for the psychic work. This meant using his fingers psychically to open a hole or incision in a person's flesh, placing fingers inside the body of the patient, all while they are completely conscious. He remembered his grandmother having done this as well.

As we ate dinner, Ambrosio told us that he had just returned from two months in Russia where people had sponsored him to do healing work. This meant that they brought in clients, maybe 5, maybe 10, maybe 15 a day. Each one paid a fee for the healing session. Even though it had been good money, when they asked him to stay longer, Ambrosio was tired and decided to return to his family. He has four grown children and a five-year-old daughter who he is anxious to watch grow up.

Then he told us the sad story of how he had experienced a series of strokes, seven in all. The worst had left him unable to walk for a year and even after much work, he now walked with a debilitating limp. Of course one would always ask why a healer would be affected by a health problem. Surely they could heal themselves? That, of course, is not the case. Though Ambrosio did receive spiritual healing from others, and this is probably the reason he is now doing so well. For someone who has had seven strokes, other than his affected gait and a slight stiffness in one arm, he appeared to be doing pretty well.

Then he became still and serious for a moment, as if he had something very important to relate and had been waiting for the right moment to share. What he would say next would be words that I probably will be contemplating for the rest of my life....

He said that he knew that when Robert contacted him after all these years, it was a sign. He knew it was of great importance. He had always known that one day he would want to pass "The Gift" to someone who would carry on the work, just as his mother and grandmother had done before him. With his ailing health, he knew that time was coming soon. Plus, he had a fairly recent addition to his family and wanted to concentrate his time on his young daughter. He said that after he got Robert's email, he started to think that the person Robert was bringing would be "The One." He believed that he had been given confirmation from Spirit that this was so. He was certain he had found "The One"–The One to carry on his tradition–The One that he could pass his gift of healing to.

...Could that person really be me?

CHAPTER 6

Passing "The Gift"

I questioned whether it was even something you could pass on. After all, were you not born with "The Gift"? Yes, he had trained as a healer, but he was born into it. It was in his lineage from his grandmother to his mother and then to him. And who knows, maybe even before that. He was also born in this magical part of the world where so many of the healers are from, as if it is an energy carried in the air or the ground. But I was not born here, and I was not even Filipino.

"Yes, but you already are a healer. You already pass the energy," he said. He continued saying that this is why he knew it would be me. After all, I was already doing the work. "Maybe you don't even need the psychic surgery part. Maybe you don't even need to open the body, but you carry the energy," he reaffirmed. He was sure he could initiate me. He was sure I would be open and connected enough to receive. It wasn't about the training. Training you could give anyone. It was about the vessel that could carry "The Gift." He had the inclination that it was me beforehand, but as soon as he met me, he was certain. He was sure he could pass me "The Gift."

I was unsure. Perhaps he knew me better than myself? Perhaps he had a spirit in his ear?

"Look, when my mother died, I didn't believe in myself either." He reassured me, "We healers are our worst enemies. Always the one that will not believe, will be yourself."

But why did he feel the need to pass this on? From the way he was talking it seemed that it was a final chapter for him. He didn't seem to be meaning that he could teach me and that we would both go on, that he would continue to work in the Philippines and I could take the training back to America. It didn't sound like a teacher/student relationship or something that I could teach others. In fact, teaching didn't seem to be a part of it at all.

No, it appeared that he would transfer his energy to me in a way that he would no longer do the work. Whether this was just his choice, to retire knowing his gift would continue through me, or whether he would somehow lose his power, I was not sure. It made me feel very sad, like a man being stripped of his powers, a man at the end of his days, giving it all up for another in a most unselfish act. Like he knew he had a powerful gift that could only be used by one person at a time and that he could no longer make so much use of it. That he would pass this torch to another who could run further and carry the light. How could I be worthy of something like that?

Was it something that I even wanted to take on? Yes, of course I would love to carry this energy and suddenly have a much more powerful gift to create healing in someone. That was a wonderful thought. Perhaps even to be able to open the body, place my hand inside, and perform miraculous healings. It was a very tempting honor. Certainly I was excited. I was thrilled that Ambrosio thought so much of me, or even more so, that he may be getting these messages about me from higher guides in the spirit world. But it was more than another technique, another string on my bow, this was a major commitment and undertaking. Would I really do it justice? He seemed certain. I was anything but sure. These next few days would reveal themselves.

We said goodnight to Ambrosio for the evening and he agreed to meet us back at the cabin in the morning. It was a perfectly adequate place for us to start the healings, and he would bring a friend he could demonstrate on.

Robert and I decided to stroll around the forest paths for a short walk before we retired for the evening. It was only 6 p.m. The sun was just setting between the pine trees, and I mused over what a beautiful spot spirit had brought us to. There was something truly magical in the air. Robert and I were still soaking in the conversation of the evening and the potential impact it might have. Robert was stunned and saddened at the health of his friend, but even more stunned by the revelation he had brought to dinner about the passing of "The Gift." On the other hand, he was thrilled for me. "This is marvelous. This is going to be amazing for you and you are the right person. This is absolutely meant to be," Robert encouraged me.

Of course, there was always the potential that "The Gift" could have been meant for Robert. Robert soon shot that down. He was set with the life he has and was not about to start a new career as a psychic healer himself. Plus, he said that he was "getting on in years." All indications pointed to a major change in my life.

No more than 10 minutes had gone by and Robert was anxious to get back and go to bed. But it was only 6:15 p.m.! Nevertheless, Robert could barely stand. "My head is buzzing like crazy. Is yours?" Robert was feeling the exact same sensation he'd had when he had visited Ambrosio 15 years earlier. After each healing day, he had staggered back to his room, his head buzzing like a "swarm of locusts" and hit the sack and was out. Tonight was no different. And yet he hadn't even worked on us. Could just being around him have this affect?

I, too, was feeling something, but I couldn't really explain it. It was like I was in some kind of spiritual veil–a sense of serenity, peace, and relaxation. Tiredness yes, but more like waves of love. Definitely a change in the energy around me. There were moments that this love was so strong that tears streamed down my face, and I became overwhelmed. As I thought of Ambrosio, I felt tremendous love for a man that I had just met, like that of spending years with a great mentor that you adore. I had a feeling of reconnection and loss all at the same time. How could I take "The Gift" from this beautiful soul and leave him with nothing? But how could I not honor such a proposition also? I felt very emotional. I was sobbing to myself feeling happy, sad, and even a little silly for crying, but Robert was zonked out and no one was there to notice.

We were sharing a room and Robert was fast asleep in the bed next to mine. I was driven to start writing down the events of this trip, lest I forgot the details. I was tired and floaty, yet I had the desire to write. Something was driving me to write everything down now, as if I could better deliver while in this spiritual veil. So I got out my computer and started typing. I was in the zone, in the moment carried away with my thoughts, and typing at top speed, when my flow was suddenly broken by Robert.

He sat up, suddenly moaning and groaning in agony to himself, clearly in a lot of pain. Was he having a nightmare? He was holding his head between his hands and screeching out as if it was aching badly. Was he in a dream? It didn't look like it. It certainly looked real. Was he receiving a strange healing from spirit? Or was something more "normal" suddenly bothering him and should I go to his aid as a healer? I offered to help, but he said he was ok and carried on in severe pain. I felt helpless. I knew it was something to do with meeting Ambrosio. Robert had been too affected by the energy for it not to be related. I knew it must be something spiritual. Still, it was hard not to be able to do anything.

Then a thought crossed my mind. Was he, in fact, the one receiving "The Gift"? Was he receiving this amazing spiritual ability? Was he being given it, right now? It certainly could have been a massive spiritual download. That might explain what was happening to him. But if he was being given "The Gift" that meant it wasn't for me after all, it was for Robert! I felt a little sad and envious for a moment. Okay, who am I kidding, I was insanely jealous. *What! I thought I was supposed to get it. Is he getting it instead?* I didn't jump at the opportunity quick enough, so now they were going to give it to Robert! *No, I'm sorry, I really did want it. Didn't you hear that Robert didn't want it anyway? I do want it!*

Robert screeched out again holding his head in agony and bending double, sitting up in bed. Seeing him in excruciating pain, I thought if this was a transfer of "The Gift," perhaps I didn't want it after all. Robert wasn't having a good time. I offered to help, but Robert just groaned, "No, I'm ok." Whether it was a healing or downloads, I presumed it was something spiritual and so much stronger than anything I could offer. I just let him know that I was just there with a little sympathy if he needed anything.

He settled down and I went back to writing on my computer. These "episodes" happened to Robert a few more times. Each time I stopped, went to him and offered help, but I was pretty useless. I wasn't even sure if he was really conscious and would even remember in the morning. Still, I was convinced that it was something to do with Ambrosio, something spiritual and therefore probably good for him even though it didn't look very pleasant.

I stayed up for a while and wrote on my computer. I felt the spirits were around, communicating with me and through my words. I talked to spirit while I was writing and asked if I was to get "The Gift" or if it had already gone to Robert. I was told in no uncertain terms that I was getting it. But was this something I was worthy of, or even wanted? I was told to see how I felt over the next few days. All would be revealed. I was just asked to have an open heart and off I went to sleep.

I was awakened just before dawn and had the inclination to be in the forest as the sun rose. I left my room and found a beautiful spot on a stump to sit and meditate for a while. I prayed for the events of the day to come. I prayed to have an open heart. It was a beautiful morning, not too hot, not too cold. I felt spirits around me. First my loved ones came and then others. A Filipino lady came to me in spirit and held my hands. Her name was Ester. The energy was beautiful. I wasn't sure whether she was giving me a healing or passing on healing powers.

I contemplated "The Gift" and how I really felt about it in my heart of hearts. I could hear a song playing ever so quietly in the distance; either that or it was playing in my head. It was a song I love by John Legend that goes, "I give you all of me, and you give me all of you..." But this time, it hit me more deeply and emotionally than ever before. I felt my heart open and, for that moment, I knew the meaning of "I give you all of me." I gave complete surrender to the day. I sat there for some time, just taking it in before returning to the cabins.

We had plenty of time to enjoy the morning, have an American Filipino breakfast, and still have time to meditate some more in preparation for our big healing day. Robert wasn't sure himself what had happened the night before. I learned that he was actually a diabetic, and it could have been a high blood sugar incident. Still, it could have been a spiritual download or a combination of the two. He really didn't know, only that he'd had a "hell of a night." Could just talking to Ambrosio have done this to him? Apparently when he had seen him years before similar, strange tiredness and other aches had been foremost.

Ambrosio arrived with his wife (partner), Nicole, as his helper and her friend Emmi, who had agreed to have a demonstration healing on camera. We set the cabin up as a makeshift healing room with a simple massage table and used a sheet that Ambrosio had brought. He didn't appear to need much. He placed a Bible on the side, then some cotton wool and cloths and a bowl, which he filled with water for washing his hands. I asked if he needed a candle, some sage, or something else. He said that the Bible was enough.

He asked for the directions of the room. He explained that it was best to position the table so that the person lay down with their head either to the north or the east. The bed was positioned along the east-west line. He explained that the energy would come into the room from the east, going into the patient's head, and then running down their body in a westward direction, moving the energy down the body from the head to the feet. This would give him a natural energy flow that would assist him. So as he worked with the energy, he would be working with the natural flow of the land. He said that moving the energy from the north to the south would also work well. The room now set up and we were ready to experience a psychic surgery session. Ambrosio had agreed to let us film all of this.

CHAPTER 7

Comatose by the Energy

Before the session started, Ambrosio and I talked a little about psychic healing on camera to recap some of the things I had learned the evening before at dinner. We talked about how Ambrosio prepares before he starts the healing. He had shared earlier, that he calls in his mother from spirit. He feels her gentle energy coming to him to work through him and he feels her holding his hands. Then perhaps he might communicate with other spirits. When he feels his spirit helpers around him, he says a prayer to God. This sounded very similar to the way I prepare to do Reiki or energy healing.

He said that he often asks his patients to pray as well. He explained that it is important that they be open to receive the energy and have faith in their healing.

Ambrosio was brought up Catholic but was "not practicing," he said. He had developed his "own prayer and own connection" as he put it. That he felt God within him and with him, always, wherever he went. He did say that wherever he is in the world, he goes into a church. Even if there was no Christian church. He said that it didn't matter that it was still a "church," whether it be a temple or mosque, whatever religion, it was still a place he felt he could talk to God.

"It's all the same thing. It's all one God," he remarked.

"It doesn't matter what God you pray to, or what religion you are, all can receive the healing." He noted that Muslims were amongst the easiest to heal. "When you ask them to pray, they really do!" he said. "They pray in a way that is devout and without question, because that is how they have learned to pray."

We talked about how the healing actually works. We talked about his beliefs, which included recognition that we have energy bodies or auras around us. He seemed to work from the principle of energy flow through us and energy centers or chakras. I noticed there was a lot of attention to the energy flow within the body and where energy might get stuck. Moving energy around, increasing flow and working on the chakras to increase the energy circulating.

From doing this work he is of the opinion that there is a physical body and then an outer invisible spiritual body around us. But then in-between the physical and the spiritual bodies there is something else. This "something else" is the area he needs to penetrate for the healing. "This might be the soul, I suppose," he said. "Something, anyway."

This seemed to be the key area for healing. It was in this Soul layer that he believed change could be made and "miraculous" results could be obtained. He explained that when you go into the physical body you have to go through and penetrate this "Soul Body" and that is where the healing is done. That this is the reason and purpose for accessing the physical body in a psychic healing because it, in some way, penetrates and heals the "soul body."

That when the body opens in a psychic surgery it is not only opening the body on a physical level but it is going through and accessing this Soul Body.

He said all ailments whether physical or emotional are held as an energy disturbance in this Soul Body. In this realm between our physical body and spiritual body. It is here that the energy needs to be realigned or redistributed to enable it to return to a healthy state.

"Sometimes the soul gets detached as well." He announced like it was a proven fact. "Like when a child gets a fever. Usually it's because they have been out playing and left their soul somewhere."

I was looking a little quizzical at this point.

"Yes, most mothers here, know this and they will go to the place where the child was playing and take a shirt or something. Then they will call the soul and ask it to come back into the shirt. When the mother takes the shirt home and puts it on the child, he will be well again."

"Oh," I said. It seemed like a lot for my western mind to take in right now.

He continued, "Children are still angels so their soul easily detaches. When we grow up it is more securely attached, and we don't lose it so easily. Unless you were in, say, a bad car accident where there is a sudden jolt then the soul can be ejected. That is why if there is an accident I go to the scene if I can, to do the healing. So I can find the soul and call it back in." This is all a whole lot for me to grasp.

Then we were right into it and Emmi was on the table being prepared for a psychic surgery. I was amazed at how quick this was happening. I had expected loads of preparation work, a ton of prayers and instruction to us, the audience. No, in a matter of minutes Emmi was prepped, her clothes pulled up and down with cloths tucked in like a surgery area prepped and ready for any blood that might be spilled. I stood next to Ambrosio to witness the entire thing. Nicole was ready, cotton swabs at hand, like a nurse waiting to assist her doctor. Robert was holding the video camera.

Ambrosio put his hand on the Bible for a moment. Then he started with a prayer no more than a minute or so. It was in Tagalog and I heard her name Emmi and the word Christo. It was clearly a prayer of petition to spirit with Catholic overtones. It had a lovely spiritual sound in this beautiful language, I thought.

As soon as he started the prayers, perhaps even before, a wave came over me. It was a very definite shift that suddenly came over me. This was not unlike the feeling after having surgery at John of God. I felt tied, inexplicably tired. Light headed and with the urge to lie down. Was I feeling faint at the sight of blood? But there hadn't even been any blood yet. *Oh my God, if I am going to faint at the thought of blood, I'm not going to be very good at this, am I?* I felt very silly but I couldn't help it. I had an urgent need to lie down. I fought the urge.

Ambrosio pressed on Emmi's third eye and solar plexus in a way I thought he was directing or increasing the energy. I could feel the energy in the room, all around him and the whole healing bed area. I knew he was channeling a powerful spiritual field.

Very quickly Ambrosio started working his fingers on the girl's abdomen. They were going deeper and deeper. Were they just pressing into the soft surface flesh appearing to sink or really starting to go inside? I couldn't tell yet. Then it came, blood pooling around his fingers. *How could it work this fast?* was my immediate thought. There was no messing around, no more prayers, no more prep, he just went right to it. He had an apparent hole in the area of her sacral chakra.

I was fighting the urge to lie down, stronger now. It was like a spiritual wave of healing had come over me. Either that or some energy was so strong I couldn't keep my eyes open, couldn't stay standing. *Was I feeling faint?* I questioned. Not really. Being faint was a different feeling, plus I wasn't one to normally feel faint. Was this how Robert was feeling the night before? It must be a really strong energy. Whatever the reason, I was having a hard time standing now.

On his subject, Ambrosio pulled back his fingers and his wife assisting, covered the "wound" with a swab of cotton wool making a patch over the area. It soaked in a little blood. Leaving the cotton on the abdomen, he moved up to another spot around the Solar Plexus. He repeated the same. Working his fingers around and around for about a minute as they appeared to sink deeper and then the blood pooling around the tips. The thought did cross my mind. *Was he holding some pouch of blood between his fingertips and squeezing the blood down a thin hidden tube?* If he was, he was extremely proficient at it. I was inches away and couldn't see any sign of anything artificial. Still I was so out of it at this point I couldn't really see or concentrate on much of anything, to tell the truth.

The third point he was to make was a spiritual incision at the throat. Once again he worked his fingers down into the flesh and within a few seconds it appeared that his fingers were slipping inside and a pool of blood formed in an apparent hole of the neck.

I was fighting to keep my eyes open. They were only half open and I was spending most of my concentration on trying to stay standing. The operation before me was a bit of a blur. It was as if a spiritual veil had come over me and I wasn't able to be fully present. I actually felt like my soul had disconnected and was standing next to me. I completely didn't feel in my body at this point.

Ambrosio now used cotton wool to soak up the blood and clean the incision areas. He waved his hands as if to close the wounds. Then he swabbed with the cotton wool. Nicole was there helping him with the wound clean up. After cleaning most of the blood with cotton, he used mineral oil to clean the remaining blood in the areas of surgery. Perhaps the oil was anointed or blessed and had healing properties, I wasn't sure.

I had made it through the whole blood part but now I really had to lie down. Luckily there was a twin bed inviting me, right next to his healing table. I slinked down to the bed and lay in an almost comatose state. It felt the extremely powerful spiritual energy. So strong, I could not move a muscle but laid spread eagle out cold. It felt like I was receiving a massive down load. I lay there completely motionless. My eyes tightly closed, I couldn't have opened them if I wanted to. Although I couldn't move or say anything, really I was in a state of bliss in a strangely heightened awareness of what was going on around me. This afterwards made me think it couldn't possibly have been a fainting queasy spell. I didn't feel sick. I felt like I was being pinned down and worked on, spiritually.

Ambrosio finished up Emmi's treatment with magnetic energy work that included some massage type movements. I was passed out on the bed at this point oblivious to everything else.

Robert had caught everything on film perfectly. Including me laid out on the bed. On the video later, I noticed how the "patient" was active with her eyes open and alert, while I, the one supposedly watching, lay completely out of it, motionless, on the bed next to her.

As soon as Ambrosio had finished on the table, he turned his attention to me. He pressed his hands on my forehead and touched points on my feet. Then he charged my energy and redistributed it. It felt wonderful. Still I couldn't move or even acknowledge him. Later he told me he was doing the "magnetic healing." Finally I sat up. Still there was a spiritual veil of energy around me.

I was vertical again and ready to continue. I was a bit embarrassed and I apologized for my silliness and explained that I felt it was the healing energy I was somehow receiving already. He reassured me telling me this was a sure sign to confirm the reason for my visit. "This is why you are experiencing the energy so quickly and so strong. They want you to absorb it, feel it and understand it."

Ok I felt a little better about myself. I was composed enough to ask questions about Emmi's healing. She was only young but Ambrosio said that he was working on lifting the internal organs like the bladder and womb. "They often drop after child birth," he explained. I was lifting all the organs in that area and resetting them in their correct place. *Interesting*, I thought. Something I could do with too I admitted. I asked her if she experienced any problems in that area. She said certainly she did and in the lower back area but now she felt no discomfort whatsoever.

Ambrosio explained that in pregnancy, as the hips start to spread it pulls the soul body away from the spine. He demonstrated with his hands linked together, fingers in an interlocking prayer position as he pulled them apart slightly representing the separation. "This is when we experience pain. The soul needs to be locked in tight," he said, demonstrating with his fingers tightly interlocking together. "It should be firm against the spine like this. When it is separated from the spine and pulled apart it hurts us physically. This is why we experience pain as the soul is being torn away." He explained in their country, during pregnancy, the women tie a scarf around their abdomen to lift it and keep the hipbones from spreading. This helps to keep it all together apparently, including the soul!

CHAPTER 8

Receiving My First Psychic Surgery

Robert was next on the table. Since he was my cameraman, this meant I would have to film it. Perhaps holding the camera would disconnect me to the energy of the event and I would feel it less. I hoped this would be the case and braced myself.

Robert was hoping for a healing of his diabetes. Something he had been sorely reminded of the night before. "Can we heal that?" he asked

"We can try," replied Ambrosio.

This always seemed to be the answer. Even though he might have had success with an ailment many times previous, he never said, "Yes, for sure." It was always just humbly, "We can try."

Robert got himself comfortable on the massage table and was prepped. I was holding the camera, something I had little experience with, but I did my best. I was feeling fairly present and able to do this now. Ambrosio said a prayer, which included Robert's name. Christo and I think something about the pancreas and diabetes. No sooner had the prayers started, I felt the wave of energy hit me again. *Oh no* I thought, *Hang on. You need to stay upright. You need to film this.* This was unbelievable. One minute I felt fine and as soon as Ambrosio started to run the energy I was totally overcome. I tried my best to stay present.

Ambrosio did the magnetic or energy healing on Robert. He placed his hands firmly on points on Robert's body and made several rubbing motions as if to circulate the energy. Then again very quickly, the surgery began. Ambrosio felt Robert's bare abdomen.

Ambrosio washed his hands in the bowl and then holding his two middle fingers together he prepared to work on Robert psychically. He chose a spot then started to work his fingers in as he had previously done on Emmi. Right away the blood pooled. He spread his fingers making a tear in his skin obscured by the blood. Then he chose two other places to create psychic surgery holes on Robert.

To be honest I wasn't fully watching, I was concentrating on holding the camera straight and trying to dispel the urge to lie down. The energy was very strong now and I was having a really hard time holding the camera. *Please hurry; I need to lie down,* I thought to myself. He finished with the incisions and started some of the magnetic healing. That was it for me. I turned off the camera and slumped back onto the bed. I landed like a sack of potatoes, laid out like I couldn't move if my life depended on it. My eyes were closed solid. Energy was buzzing wildly through my head. Now I knew what Robert meant by the "swarm of locusts running through your brain."

Ambrosio was busily working on Robert still and it was as

if I could feel every movement. I was lying on the bed with my eyes closed yet I seemed to be aware of every movement Ambrosio was doing. He finished the session with Robert then once again Ambrosio turned to give me the magnetic energy. In my case it was about giving me the energy to sit up. Finally I was able to sit. Ambrosio brought me a glass of water. Water of course was to flush out the overload of energy I was receiving. "Drink this, this will help to move the energy through you." After a few minutes, shaky and not all together there, I was at least able to converse again.

Ambrosio seemed quite proud this was happening to me; "This is you receiving the energy downloads," he said with a satisfied smile. Then he went on to talk on camera about how he was sure that I had come so he could pass this Gift to me. A rush of love came through me and I became very emotional, tears streaming down my face. I was still in this energy veil and I was feeling heightened emotions. We hugged and he too streamed tears. "We should both be happy," he said, trying to break the ice.

"I am very happy," I assured him. It was one of those times that you cry with love and emotion over something beautiful and profound. It was a moment we will both never forget.

It was time for me to experience receiving a psychic surgery. This would be my first psychic surgery like this and I must admit there was some fear. I asked Robert if it hurt, hoping he would say not.

"I could feel the cut but it was like a nick like when you cut yourself shaving. You can feel it but it doesn't hurt," assured Robert.

I got up on the table and was prepped. My trousers rolled down to my hips and lined with a cloth and my top pulled up to my breasts also lined. My abdomen was exposed and ready for "surgery." Whether I was being given a spiritual anesthetic or not, I was not sure, as I was already severely drunk with spiritual influence.

Still there was a moment of fear that someone was about to open up my body. I tried to calm myself. I tried to concentrate on the thought that it could be fake. If I could convince myself it was fake, then that would make me not so scared. Then I got upset with myself for lack of faith and that this might impede anything I was supposed to be receiving. *Just open your heart, Gail, and receive what you are meant to. And TRUST!* I thought to myself.

Ambrosio said his prayers and all fear seemed to dissolve into pure love and acceptance. Ambrosio started with the magnetic healing and I felt the flow of energy around my body. I could feel his fingers like magnets pulling energy from one place to another.

Then the psychic surgery began. I was as relaxed and in bliss as I could have been. I just felt pressure. There was a slight cutting sensation. It could have been the feeling of a psychic opening. It could have been the feeling of the skin opening, but it could have also been the feeling of a fingernail running along my flesh. I really couldn't say. My eyes were closed so I wasn't so scared. In fact there was a beautiful feeling of love. As if someone was smiling down on me. Whatever was happening physically I didn't know but on a spiritual level there was a huge veil of spiritual healing around me. It was like thousands of beautiful higher guides were directing healing energy over my entire body. It passed through me, along me like waves of love. It seemed to flow through my head, down my body to my feet. The abdomen "surgery" was complete. I knew now that there were probably two more areas coming. That was what I was expecting and that is what I got.

After he "closed" the wounds and "cleaned" them he continued the Magnetic healing or energy work. As he spread the energy over me, this felt like a super nice massage. Like a physical massage but also at the same time, a deep energy massage. *Oh, I could have an hour of this,* I thought. He did what I would learn later was the spreading of the energy.

Then he worked on my abdomen massaging and lifting the organs. That was a little strange. Not really painful. I had just a little discomfort. It was as if he was massaging my womb back up my body. He slid his hands inside my pants at either side of my public bone pulling up the flesh. On camera it looked a little invasive but it didn't feel it at all. It really felt that all my organs were being lifted and repositioned. He had me bend my knees to enable him to get deeper into my abdomen.

Then he spread the energy uniformly throughout my body and I could feel it running smoothly down me. He ended the session, by having me sit up and face away from him. He grabbed my shoulders and placed his forehead in the back of my spine. I could feel his third eye pulsating energy into the center of my back. Pulling my shoulders towards him as his head firmly pressed into my spine. It was a sort of stretching of the shoulders and pushing into the spine, all in one. There was definitely a transfer of energy from his head to my Kundalini.

The whole session felt like I was receiving love. From him and a thousand healers in spirit. It felt like he truly cared about me. Like the whole universe loved me. I thanked him for the amazing experience and told him how wonderful it felt.

Ok, that would be it for today's session. That had been more than enough mind blowing for one day! He would come back and give both Robert and I healings for the next two days and my initiation would start. On the third day he would give me an official initiation and passing of his energy.

Bali, island of mysteries and dreams.
Temple of "The Rock and The Sea" behind me.

A fun reading from Ketut
(Eat Pray Love)

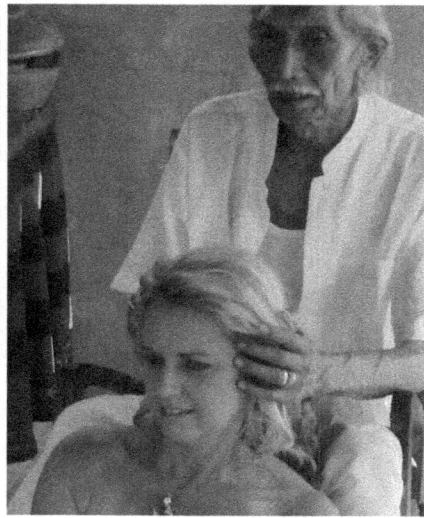

Cadoka, the healer doing
the mysterious jaw adjustment

Anthony the Healing Angel

Meditating in Baguio Woods

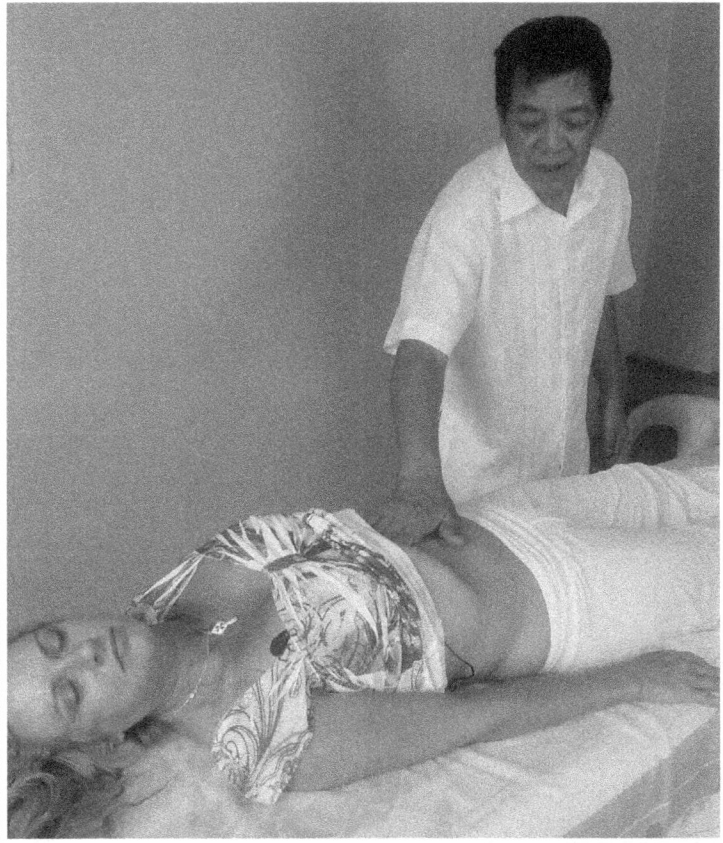

Ambrosio prepares for my first surgery

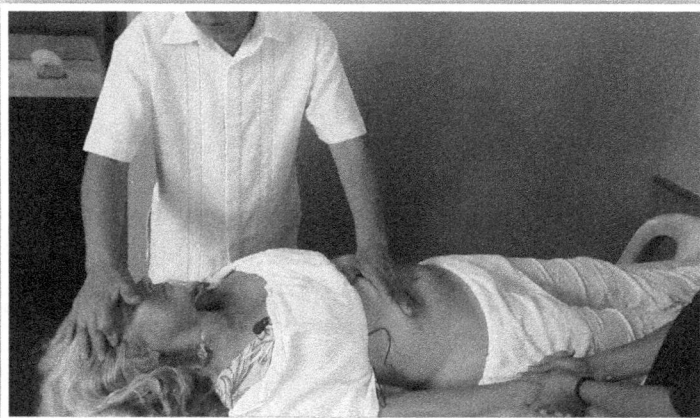

Ambrosio does magnetic healing

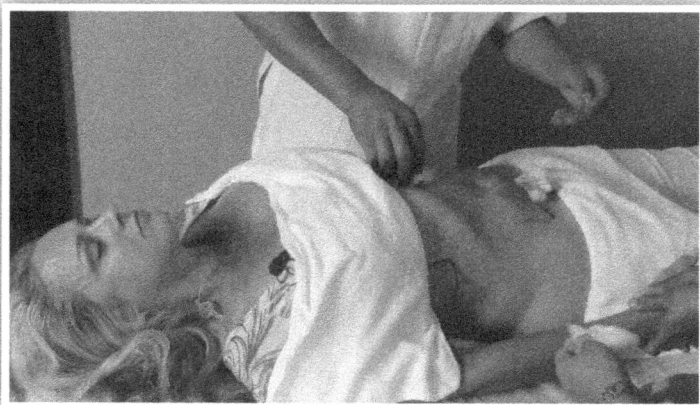

Ambrosio performs psychic surgery on me

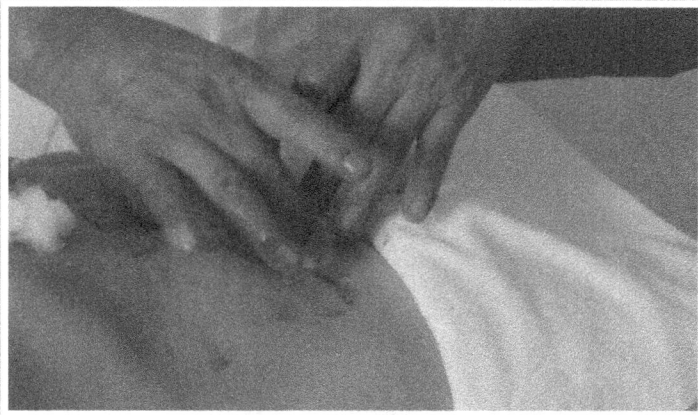

Ambrosio makes psychic cut

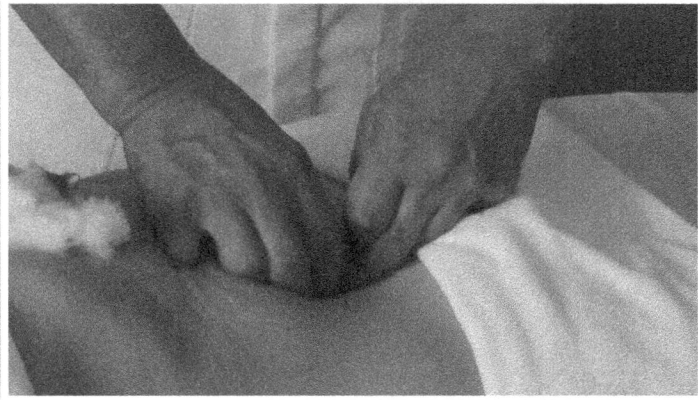

Ambrosio inserts his finger

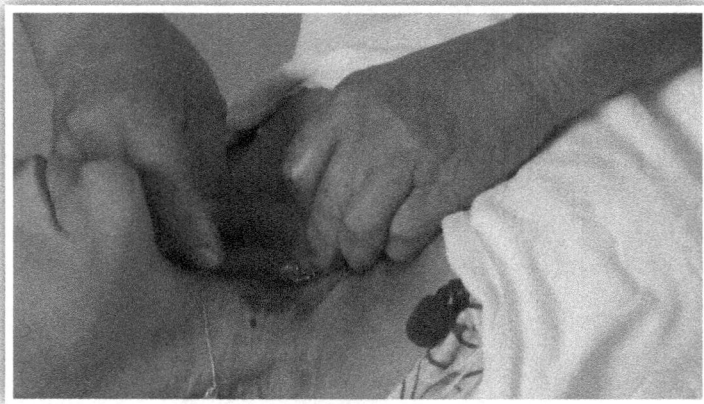

Throat psychic surgery

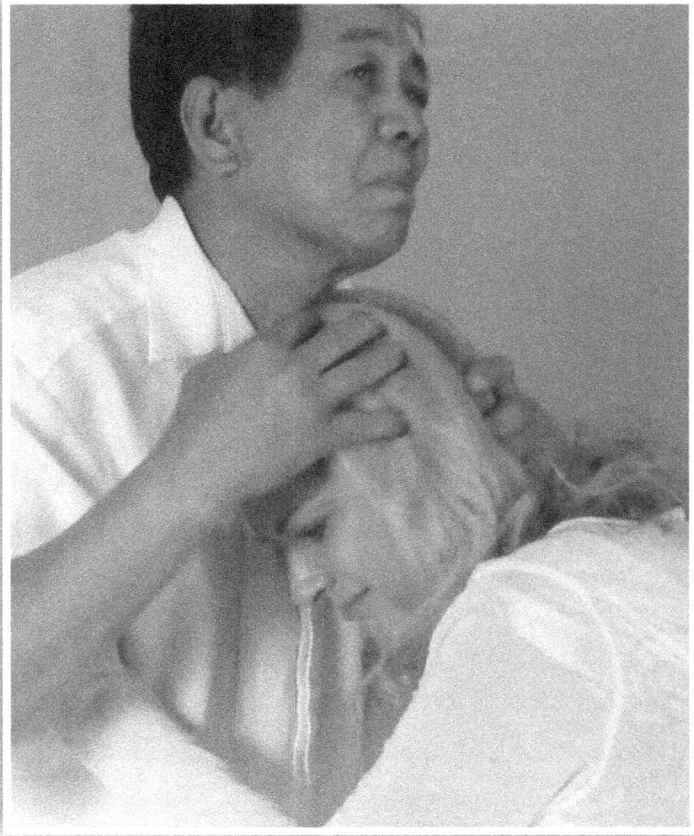

A touching moment as Ambrosio
tells me he will pass me "The Gift"

The birth mark – just in front of his left ear.

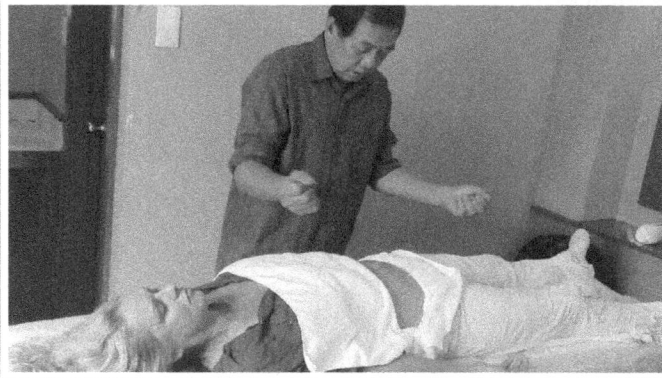

Ambrosio prepares to pass The Gift

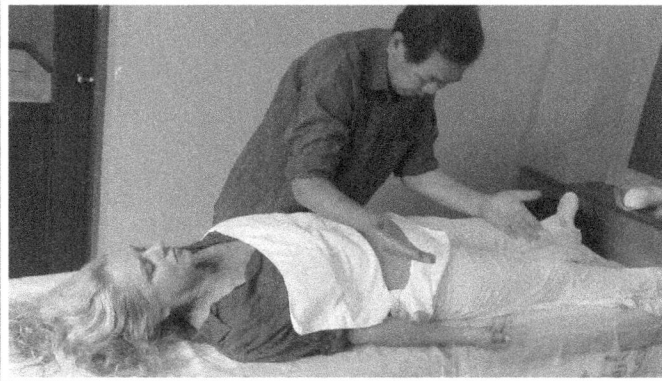

Ambrosio imparts his energy

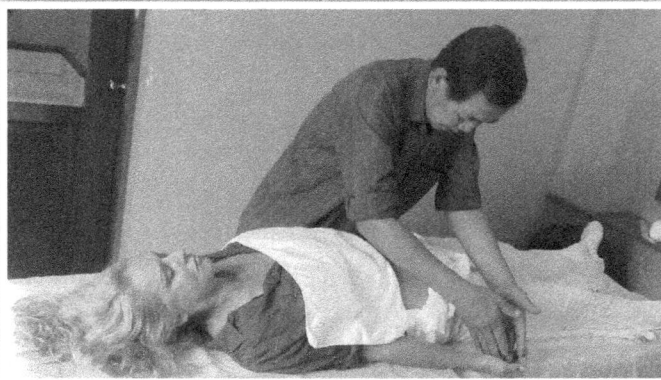

Ambrosio opens my palm chakra

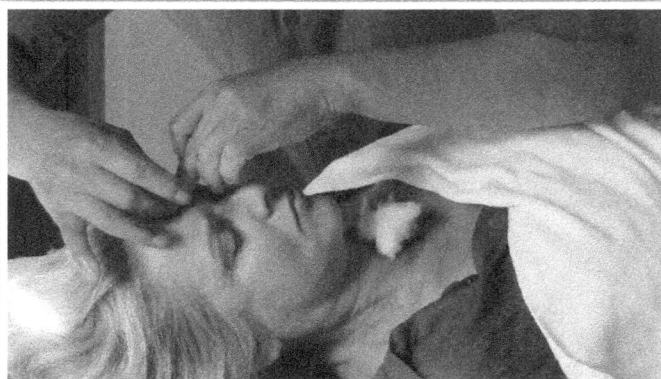

Opening of the third eye chakra

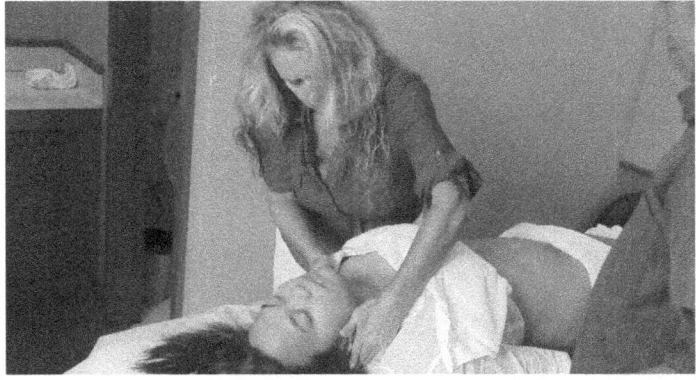

Learning to perform Magnetic Healing

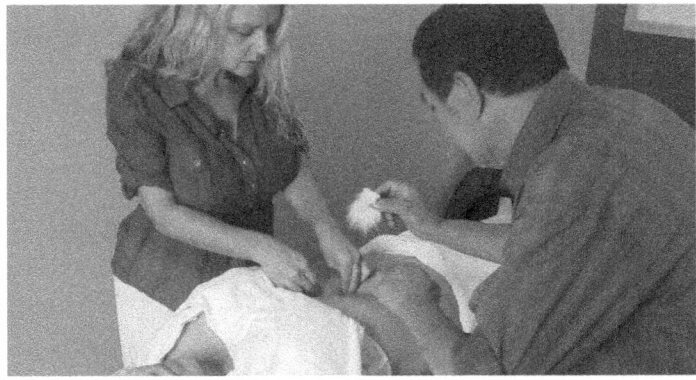

Learning psychic surgery

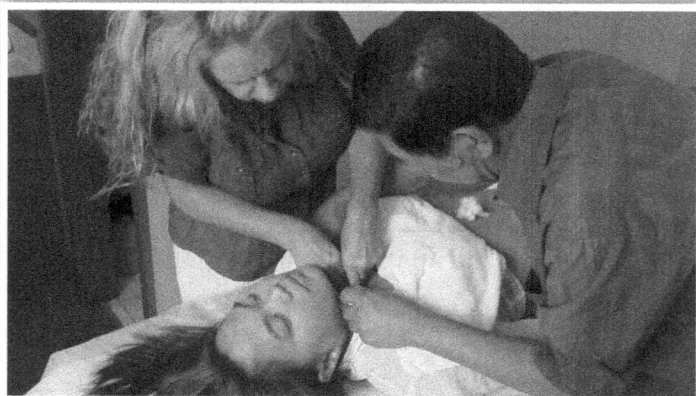

Me doing surgery on Nicole

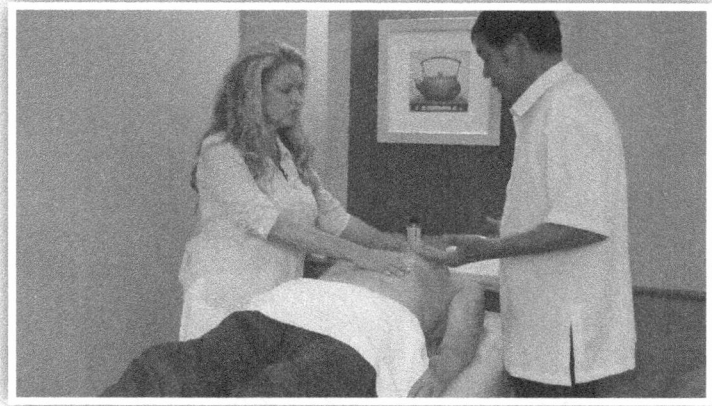

Calling in the energy

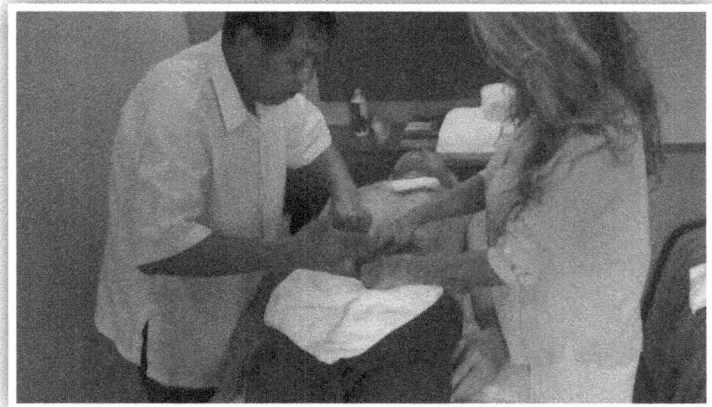

Opening the body

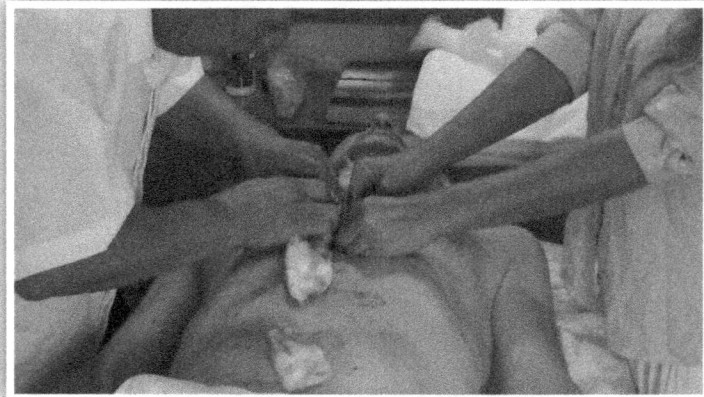

I'm performing psychic surgery!

CHAPTER 9

Past Life Connection

We all went off for some lunch together. Both Robert and I were clearly out of it still. Going along with everyone else, just trying to put one foot in front of the other. We had a nice lunch and chatted about the healing but also other more mundane things. Ambrosio sat opposite me and I was somewhat focused curiously but almost subconsciously on a mark just in front of his left ear. Finally my contemplation was broken as Robert brought it to everyone's attention. Robert remarked that the birthmark on the side of Ambrosio's face was probably an indication of a past life incident.

Oh, my God!!! It finally dawned on me! You know when something triggers you and you are suddenly reminded of a dream? It had been on the long bus ride up in one of those half asleep, half-awake times that I had a "dream." But I knew at the time, it wasn't a dream at all, it was a past life vision.

Spirit had been trying to remind me of my past life vision all day and I finally got it. In the morning they had tried to remind me when a young man passed by us. I remarked to Robert about the big bruise on the boy's face. Robert said that he thought it could be a birthmark, and we got into a whole conversation about how birthmarks could show where you were killed in a past life. That should have triggered it for me but it hadn't.

Then there could have been the signal from spirit as we were sitting at the lunch table when I asked Ambrosio if he knew his past lives. "Just wondering if you remember being a healer in a past life?" I was just curious.

He said he didn't remember his, but three different psychics had told him that he was a doctor in a past life. Even then, the spirits didn't get me to remember.

Staring obliviously at the mark on Ambrosio's cheek wondering about it didn't remind me either.

But now Robert hit me over the head with it and spirit final got the message across. I was finally reminded of my vision.

I had "dreamt" that I was in some time period long ago, in a place that was Inca or perhaps Indonesian. I was in power, a queen or something (but possibly a man I hadn't asked). There was a great plague that had devastated my people. When I asked what, my spirits simply said, "passed by flies." Whatever it was, it was a terrible disease that had rampaged our small village and affected the young and old alike. The doctor from the village was standing helplessly forlorn, in front of me.

"What type of doctor? A medical doctor or a spiritual healer?" I asked my spirit guides.

"There was only one kind back then. It was the same thing, a doctor."

"Oh yes of course." I felt a little silly for asking that.

I had much sympathy for the doctor, though I am not sure

I was allowed to show it. Many lives had been lost, and he felt completely helpless. He felt like he had failed at his mission. I was devastated about the loss, but I wanted to let him know that it wasn't his fault and that some things are beyond any of us. I wanted to help with the healing in some way, but he was the only one qualified, the only one who had the gift of healing bestowed by the gods. I wanted to be there to help my people, but I wasn't able. I didn't know how and even my doctor couldn't help them.

The people were angry and scared. This doctor had the healing gift from the gods, so if he couldn't remove the plague, then he must be out of favor with the gods. I knew the doctor felt afraid, but even more, that he felt like a failure. I knew that the doctor would pass to the next life feeling this guilt of not being able to save these people—a feeling of failure. It was a feeling that his healing mission was not complete. I knew this would show up in his future lives, and I had a feeling that he would be with me in this life.

"How will I recognize this doctor?" I asked my guides.

"You will see him by the mark of how he was killed in his previous life, by the birthmark just in front of his left ear. This is how you will recognize the doctor."

With that, the vision faded. I wasn't sure why I had seen this or who this was. It didn't seem to relate to anything in my life and I had no idea who the "doctor" could be. It didn't seem to be anyone I recognized. And why did I have this spontaneous Past Life regression? It was not like I was in the habit of having these. Even for me, this was highly unusual. Then I must have forgotten about the vision as it settled somewhere in my subconscious.

Now, finally today, it all came together for me. Sorry spirits I see you have been showing me all day. So Ambrosio was the doctor in my vision! Wow! Now I realize I had been shown a vision and that vision had been confirmed. In a big way! But still I didn't know why. This was too much synchronicity not to be relevant but what was the significance? Just to show me that we had a past life together? To show me why he had this healing mission in this life? I wasn't sure yet.

Robert and I could barely keep our eyes open.

"You guys might want to rest a little," Ambrosio said.

Bloody right. What were we even thinking, walking into the village for lunch? We were wiped out. We said goodbye and Robert and I made our way back to the hotel. It was only about a block but uphill. It was the longest, hardest, block I had made in my life. We both groaned and moaned and regretted having walked down in the first place. We were holding each other up dragging each other. We finally made it back to the hotel to crash.

"I am completely wacked. He did a number on me today. I feel like I was hit over the head with a sledgehammer.... But in a good way," Robert said, falling headfirst flat out on the bed.

I felt the same way. An energy buzzing in my head and without the strength to move a muscle. This was crazy. It was so strong we could barely drag ourselves around. It was amazing to both of us that a spiritual healing like this could have such a strong affect.

"Do you think it's completely real?" I asked. I mean, was he holding a tube of blood or something or was this really happening? I thought it was real but wasn't one hundred percent convinced. Robert had very little doubt.

"I couldn't see anything in his hands but he holds them strange. Is that just a technique?" I asked Robert. Robert noted that when he came before, Ambrosio held his fingers differently using his index fingers together and then spreading them apart. "Then you could totally see there was nothing there." But now he held his hands differently. Perhaps because he had a stroke. Was there any trickery here we both wondered.

But what were we talking about. How could we even be thinking that way? The two of us could barely walk. There was no mistaking it; it wasn't subtle at all. We could both barely stand. Clearly something had hit both of us like a ton of bricks and yet we were asking was this real? Well something was completely real! We both agreed this could definitely not be in our mind. This was real!

It was about 1 p.m. We both collapsed on the bed and literally passed out. Robert didn't experience any strange painful awakenings this time, thank goodness. And I was too zonked to do anything anyway. We both fell into an immediate deep sleep. Neither of us stirred for a good six hours. Even then, it was only for a quick bite and then we crashed again. Robert tried to hold a cup of coffee but was too weak and spilled it down himself. To say we had received a massive dose of spiritual healing was an understatement.

I woke sometime just around sunset and went outside to meditate. I went to do some healing work on others back home. *I really hope they feel some of this.*

I used some sticks and pinecones I found lying around, called in my spirit guides and began distance healing work. I had my eyes closed but I distinctively felt someone to my right. I carefully opened my eyes expecting that there would be no one there, just spirit energy I was feeling. But there was someone else there; there were two sets of eyes looking at me. They belonged to two house cats, both white and ginger colored. They were intently staring at me. When I looked back at them, they acted as if they were working with me and had suddenly been caught. They continued staring for a second and then slicked off nervously as if they had been caught in the act. Strange, I thought, I hadn't seen any cats the whole time I'd been here.

I closed my eyes and continued my focus. After I finished, I opened my eyes. Just a few feet in front of me was yet another cat. Also, white and ginger, she could have been one of the pair, but they had taken off in another direction. She was staring at me. I know she had been there a long time, but once I broke the energy she quickly and nervously left. *Yes this is a very special place.*

I went inside and passed out in an almost spiritually driven sleep. I think I woke and wrote some more on my computer but if I did it was in a semi-asleep state.

Robert and I woke nice and early and went to the American 50s diner for a good ol' American breakfast–a slice of Americana in Baguio. Robert was much more awake this morning. Well, he should have been, he'd had like 35 hours sleep in the last 48 hours. I did a little meditation to prepare again for the day, before Ambrosio and Nicole arrived.

CHAPTER 10

Wow, Here
We Go Again

It was a beautiful day again and I took an early morning stroll among the pine trees. I did some meditation and I asked the land if I could pick some pinecones to take home with me. I thought surely they carry the energy of these great trees and this beautiful place.

Ambrosio and Nicole arrived refreshed and ready to get right into the work. Robert was up first. He hopped on the massage table and the healing began. Ambrosio worked over Robert in a very similar way to the day before. He had said that for most people three sessions in a row would be beneficial, to really get a complete healing. Presumably Ambrosio was working on the same issues for Robert.

As soon as he began the prayers, once again I was being given a dose of the spiritual veil. *Oh wow! Here we go again!*

Perhaps it would be slightly less today. Perhaps if I concentrated really hard, I could stand it. Ambrosio appeared to open Robert in similar areas as he had operated on him, the day before.

I was filming, getting a little more used to holding the camera and this time being conscious of keeping myself out of the mirror reflection. Pleasantly, I was a little more used to the energy too and although it still felt extremely strong, I wasn't quite as bad. I couldn't really focus on what was happening but at least I didn't have to lie down until after Robert's session was finished.

I tried to focus on the physical healing. What exactly was going on? Ambrosio held his fingers in a specific way as if the middle fingers were instruments and the rest needed to stay out of the way. Was it real? It certainly looked real but I couldn't be completely sure. I couldn't see anything in Ambrosio's hands and I got a good look at all his fingers. The blood I was convinced was completely real. But were his fingers actually going inside Robert's body? Perhaps is was just the tips.

Then it was my time for my second healing. Again mine felt very similar. A warm flow of love came over me. He worked on my front, then cleaned me off, turned me over and did the spreading of the energy over my back. Then back to the front side. Massaging my organs up in my abdomen and continuing with a very nice massage of the energy down my legs. I kept my eyes closed. One, because to be honest I didn't want to see any blood and freak out, and two, because I felt that would be better for my healing if I wasn't consciously watching and questioning everything.

Then today there was a little addition I was not expecting. My eyes were closed shut but Ambrosio leaned over and opened my right eye lid wide. Of course I could see him looking in at me. *"Oh, he's going to work on my eyes."* I thought. I had mentioned my eye sight at lunch yesterday as I grabbed my glasses to read the menu.

What I didn't expect was the way he was going to work on them. The next thing I saw was as he leaned over me his tongue was out. *Oh no, he is coming towards me with his tongue. He is not going to stick his tongue in my eye is he? Surely not!* Oh yes, that's exactly what he did.

He stuck his wet tongue into my open eye, forcing it all around my eyeball and giving it a thoroughly good licking.

Aw, yuk! I must admit was my thought. Then of course he had to do the other eye. Now I knew what was coming. He forced the eyelid open and sure enough stuck his tongue in the other eye, forcefully licking all around the surface.

Wow! I thought. *I didn't expect that!*

That was the final procedure before he closed down the healing session. I was a little giddy and giggled. Was it from the silliness of having my eyeball licked or was it some kind of fun energy that had come in to my field?

"Do you do that often?" I inquired to Ambrosio about the licking of the eyeball.

"Oh, yes, if someone has an eye issue."

"But aren't you worried you might get an infection or something?" I said at the vision of some nasty looking eye condition walking into his clinic.

"No, it's no problem. I am spiritually protected. Never get sick from healing."

Robert chuckled. He had caught everything on camera. He had been quite in disbelief wondering exactly what he was doing. He was thinking Ambrosio was sucking my eyeball or something weird. We had a little laugh about it afterwards. We weren't sure any American client's I'd bring out would enjoy that very much.

Still I was going to be learning this healing, so Robert need not laugh, I was going to be licking his eyeball soon! This was a bit of a friendly joke for the rest of the evening. "Don't worry I'm going to be licking your eyeball!"

CHAPTER 11

Are There Fake Healers?

This morning's sessions had gone a little quicker that the day before. We knew the ropes now. We were still blasted with energy and needed to rest but not as bad as the previous day.

We all went to Starbucks for a coffee and a chat. Yes, they love America! Over a cuppa we discussed the healing a little more. And I asked about other psychic healers. I inquired if there are fake healers. If they ever add blood and guts, or fake cuts if they can't really do this.

"Are *all* the psychic surgeons here real?" I wondered. "Do any of them just fake it for the money or the fame?"

"Sure," he said, "There are those who do that."

I couldn't imagine that they could last that long, though, without someone finding out. Ambrosio had been healing for 40 years!

"But what if they can really heal, but are just not "on" that day. Would they ever fake it?" I know from my own experience that it is not always there and spirit cannot always be conjured on request. "How can they always produce results? Especially if they have these huge clinics with people lined up. What if it just doesn't work sometimes, and they have a line of people waiting?"

Ambrosio thought some did blood and guts. He said that some clients just didn't believe if they couldn't see a physical sign. I agreed. Robert and I knew Ambrosio's healing was real even without any blood. It had completely knocked our socks off. The energy was so strong it was more than obvious. But to some, especially tourists like the Japanese, they had travelled far and expected blood or they were not happy. In a way I suppose if the healing was real and they did something to the client to make him believe and make him able to be receptive to the healing, was that really deception? I mean if the end result was true healing, wasn't that the important thing?

If someone was to do this simply for the "show" or worse just to get money out of people this seemed like a despicable practice. But if someone was really healing and just added "props" to help the patient believe then it seemed justified. Still there was a fine line here.

Ambrosio said that sometimes real healers lose power to open the body and then add to it, or fake it. I could understand that the actual physical part of the healing must take tremendous energy and concentration. You could see that there could be pressure to perform on the part of the healer and if he didn't, then some might lose faith in the healing itself.

Some of the healers, he told us, only did the Magnetic Healing and were extremely powerful. His mother even only did magnetic healing. His grandmother though had done the psychic surgery and opened the body as well as the magnetic healing. Still those that only do the magnetic healing don't get as much attention.

"What about those that pull out guts and nails and other things, is that possible?"

Ambrosio told us that some things come out of the body. Some things, like nails, are sometimes manifested psychically by the healer. Perhaps a nail might be more a representative of an energy but nevertheless, it can appear as a physical object that can be removed from the body. But he thought there were some that did this as a show and it was not real at all. And there are certainly healers that have been caught with pieces of chicken guts.

I had heard of film crews doing DNA testing on the subject's blood and guts that appeared to come out of the body and they had turned out to match that of the patient. "Yes," Ambrosio agreed. "But if they are here to test DNA and try to disprove the healing, then they probably don't have the disposition to receive the healing. So I would rather not work on those people." He was correct. If someone disbelieved going in, then the lack of faith would probably prevent their healing, giving them a self-fulfilling prophecy.

It seemed that public display of psychic surgery had become more rare anyway. Practicing psychic healing at all has become more difficult. It seems healers also have to be careful. In certain countries it could be deemed "practicing medicine without a license" and punishable with jail time. Even in the Philippines now they are getting into a lot of hot water because medical doctors are now complaining that they were taking money out of their pockets. There are so many interesting things to learn. Now we need a rest.

We both felt deep love for Ambrosio and his work, however

not to take anything away from him, we wondered what the other healers in these parts were like. Did they have similar techniques? Did they do group healings and distance healings or mostly one-on-one sessions? While we were here, we might as well do some research.

So here in Baguio we inquired around town as to who were the most famous psychic healers. It seemed most did magnetic healing. In fact this seemed to be the actual necessary part of the job. Then there were those that also did the psychic surgery on top. It was this psychic surgery part of it, the actual opening of the body, that people flocked to see.

These healers were not as easy to find as we thought though. We had several names and addresses, so we figured we could find their phone numbers on the Internet—not so. How about the directory at the hotel in Baguio? That proved difficult as well. We decided to make a day of it and hired a taxi to comb the streets of Baguio…and getting totally lost. It was certainly an adventure. Apparently, the house numbers are not in any particular order. Number 22 was next to number 89 and so on. Robert remarked, "Perhaps people take their addresses with them if they move." The taxi driver also told us that there were several streets named the same in different parts of the city. Still, it was a great way to see the town, get into the back streets, and visit a few slum neighborhoods. We got to talk to lots of locals and eat food from the street carts. That probably was not wise! We had a great time but didn't find much. This was not something I would recommend doing after dark.

We did arrive at the famous Jun Lobo's house. He, apparently, is one of the most famous Filipino psychic surgeons and by all accounts, a very entertaining and colorful character, even at nearly 80-years-old. He has traveled overseas extensively and been paid by many Arabian princes. The healers that have become rich and famous seem to have gotten their celebrity status overseas. Clearly this one had money. His mansion was set back into the hill, surrounded by a high security wall topped with barbed wire. There was a guard gate and a guard dog house, containing a very big dog. It looked like what you might see in a movie depicting a Columbian drug lord's compound. We rang the bell at the guard gate. The little window slot opened up, and I smiled sweetly. We were let in. Unfortunately, Mr. Lobo was resting, and so we were invited to come back in the morning to watch the line of people that gather for his psychic surgery clinic.

Jun usually works with groups, holding morning sessions and inviting all those who wish to come. He says that he calls in Jesus to heal through him and enable him to do psychic surgeries. He leads everyone in prayer and sometime during the prayer he says he "receives the energy of the Holy Spirit." He says he also works with an Indian guide named "Rama."

The group gathers around his healing table and then Jun works on each person individually. For westerners this would look quite unusual. Most people are almost naked, perhaps just a cloth to cover them until it is their time to get up on the table.

Jun has a unique technique whereby he holds a white sheet in front of the patient to energetically "see" their ailments. This reminded me of other healers who say if we wear white they can better "read" our energy. After "reading" their energy through the cloth, he then goes to work on them energetically to remove any disease or issues that ail them.

Perhaps Jun also received his Gift from his mother. His

mother was a psychic dentist, extracting teeth and doing other dental work, without anesthetic, through psychic surgery.

The story goes that one day Jun was in church when he was suddenly paralyzed. He was very afraid. Then an apparition of Jesus came. Jesus told him he would be one of Jun's guides. Later Jun was walking with his mother and another woman when the woman collapsed. Jun instinctively placed his hands on the woman's chest. Suddenly blood appeared. Jun was terrified and fled. He had no idea what was happening. The people brought Jun back and asked him to continue healing the woman. He did and she fully returned to health. Jun has been healing ever since that day with literally thousands of people saying they have been cured by him.

We really wanted to experience a session with Jun, but we had big plans with Ambrosio tomorrow so we took a rain check. Still there is lots and lots of footage you can see on the Internet of Jun Lobos in action.

In fact, you can see on the Internet that many seem to have the same technique. They mostly seem to do magnetic healing. Then, for the psychic surgery, they hold either both their index fingers together or both their middle fingers together and then as they separate their fingers, a line or cut appears on the body.

I noticed that most worked on clients one by one, while other patients waiting could watch. However, there was usually a rope or line that the others could not cross so that they won't crowd the healer. One of the psychic surgeons explained this to us. "Yes, the energy is very high on the bed and in the healing area around the client. It is very delicate. So the rope is so that the others don't cross into the energy. This could affect the healing. But also the energy is so high that close that most people would not be able to even stand up." Wait, rewind. Ah-ha! That explains it! I wasn't imagining this. Ambrosio never mentioned it but clearly other people couldn't get close because the energy is so strong. I just stood right next to Ambrosio from the very first moment to get a bird's eye view. I was also clearly within the energy blast!

On our travels we met Nester Lobos, Jun Lobos' son, also a healer but very much doing his own thing. Nester told us he did Magnetic Healing very easily and could demonstrate very quickly for us. However the psychic surgery takes much concentration. It requires a great energy and therefore preparation time. This is also the reason most healing clinics are held in the morning when the healer has the most steam.

Brother Laurence was also to be found in Baguio. Although he apparently does psychic surgery, he seemed more focused on prevention of disease and working on diet, exercise, and addressing the emotions. He added in the use of magnets and a low voltage current device he uses for healing. I wondered if this was in a way, enhancing the magnetic healing that most seemed to do in these parts or if this was something separate.

Arsenia Terte De La Cruz was another highly recommended healer in Baguio. She is the daughter of Eleuterio Terte, who was the first ever Filipino psychic surgeon (or at least that has been recorded in modern times). However, like several others now, she only does magnetic healing.

There seemed to be about five or six pretty famous psychic healers in this area. And when I say pretty famous I mean we probably know about them because they have travelled overseas and you can find footage on the Internet. Asking the locals, there are numerous others but you really don't have a clue as to who are any good.

Some work through a church or similar organization, in which case there could be several healers associated with one church group. Spiritual churches are of the faith that spirits are around us and able to help and heal us, which are the basic principles behind psychic healing and psychic surgery. Attending services might include the usual prayers and sermons but might also include a medium or clairvoyant giving messages to the congregation. It might also include spiritual healers giving blessings and even psychic surgery.

Most healers seemed to ask for a donation for an individual session. For the more famous this seemed to be around $50 to $100. However, I presumed that this was the rate quoted to Americans as I doubted most local people could afford anything like that. I wouldn't begrudge them, though, as this is what most of them do for a living. It didn't look like many were getting rich on this anyway.

We found that almost all the healers used magnetic healing, a type of energy healing or Reiki with some added energy massage and Kundalini work. Several of them did psychic surgery but this seemed to be the more difficult and more sought after display.

Almost all that we talked to said that the healing was in the energy healing. It was this magnetic healing where the real healing took place. It was a type of a shift in consciousness, an access to the ethereal body that changed the energy of the soul body or energy body around us. Just as I had found in my own work and that of many others, the secret is in the energy body, that we store all our ailments, physically or emotionally, as a disturbance in our energy body. A spiritual healing changes the energy and restores it to the state that is of wholeness.

The psychic part of it, as it is referred to here, or the opening of the physical body, many believe is simply to help the patient to believe. Because if the patient has faith and belief in their healing, then they are open to receive and a shift in their energy is more likely to occur.

We met some other healers that had no problem being filmed doing magnetic healing but getting them to perform psychic surgery on film proved more difficult. Especially if they were back in our room, where we had more control. After we explained to one that we would be looking to make sure there was nothing fake, he changed his mind and didn't show up. We took that as an indication that he couldn't really do it. His not showing up was a shame because I really felt that he did have substantial healing powers. Again, the psychic part seemed more difficult and often just to help people to believe, while the real healing was in the energy.

Several famous psychic surgeons can be found in another town, Pangasinan, about an hour and a half south (or about three hours, depending on who you ask). These include the infamous Alex Orbito, who I know has traveled to America numerous times. In fact, my dear friend Sean was involved in some of his visits. Sean had witnessed firsthand, Orbito doing psychic surgeries. In fact, he even saw an operation performed on a friend of his where Orbito removed the guy's eyeball. Apparently, in the eye operation, he pulled the eyeball out and left it hanging on the cheek while he cleaned inside the socket, and then simply popped it back in. All of this was with no anesthetic! Sean's friend's eyesight did apparently improve after!

Sean told me something that I found particularly interesting though. Sean said that during a surgery on a person's abdomen,

Sean got down to eye level at the site of the surgery. There he saw a very strange sight. He saw a double image, one of the normal body and the other of the body penetrated. It was almost as if it was a 3-D overlay, as if the psychic surgery was taking place on another, ethereal level or in another dimension. Sean was seeing both dimensions at the same time.

Anyway, our little research adventure served to convince us that we had probably the most skilled, most impressive psychic surgeon one could find and, miraculously, he had stayed fairly out of the spotlight.

CHAPTER 12

My First Instruction

It was now our third day of healing with Ambrosio. The initiation had begun and he would start to instruct me and walk me through performing a healing. I was excited to speed things up but couldn't imagine that I was going to somehow be able to do psychic surgery myself.

Robert was up first again. This would be his third on the issue of diabetes. Robert had already forgotten to take his medication (we know in the spiritual world this is a good sign). And his blood sugar level seemed to have leveled out to fairly normal.

As we started to prep our patient Robert. Ambrosio noted that my hands were very cold. I rubbed them together to warm them so Robert wouldn't get an unpleasant shock of icy hands on his abdomen.

Ambrosio said a prayer of his own and then led me on how to pray. "Just prepare as you normally would, calling in your energy. Ask for your guides and your loved ones to be around. Ask to be connected to God or Divine Source or whatever you say. Ask to be an instrument of healing, that the healing energy will run through you and that they will use your body." Ambrosio talked me through the praying to receive the connection to spirit. I could feel an immediate rush of energy. Higher than I would normally experience. "Now concentrate on Robert. Think about his healing. Ask that his diabetes be healed and anything else that he needs." My palms and particularly my fingertips were tingling like crazy.

After the prayer I could feel the energy in the room. It was an amazing high and I was floating. I could tell my vibration was at top speed. I wondered if this was just from my prayer or if Ambrosio had somehow imparted the energy on me as he prayed with me. In other words is this something I would be able to repeat on my own? And did it also have something to do with this magical place? Either way, I was now high on spiritual energy.

Ambrosio instructed me to place my hands on Robert and feel the energy. My hands lit up like electrical beacons and I could literally feel tingles of "electricity" or some kind of current, running through them. Actually not electricity, it was a different, a more smooth and loving current. I was not completely in the room at this point. I felt I was out of my body. I was being driven and guided by spirit and felt in some way they were in control of my body.

Then Ambrosio showed me how to push down and create an energy surge in the chakras. I noticed he would keep the heart chakra connected to the third eye. Then the heart connected to the Solar Plexus and so on. This meant having both hands one over the other, both pressed firmly over the chakra and concentrating the energy into the area. I breathed the energy through me and into Robert. I could literally feel Robert's chakras spinning as I did this. It was like a gust of wind suddenly spinning a fan. Rotating in a fast and sudden spurt. Then Ambrosio had me keep the connection on the heart with one hand while the other touched the sacral chakra and so on, connecting the chakras.

After I raised a chakra and could feel it spinning, Ambrosio directed me; "Now spread the energy." Ambrosio insisted. As if the energy needed to be quickly dispersed through the body while the energy was there. He showed me how to pull the energy from the third eye and rub it firmly over Robert's head, eyes and ears. "Now take it from the heart and run it around the chest." He pressed down on the heart chakra and showed me how to build it, then to spread the energy around the chest. "Now the abdomen." I took the energy from Robert's sacral chakra just below his navel and in a circular motion distributed the energy around. I could feel it and see it circulating in his body. On Robert we also worked on the area of the Pancreas and Liver.

Ambrosio had Robert turn over and he showed me how to work on the Kundalini. He started at the point at the base of the skull where he pressed to release the energy. Then he ran the energy down the spine. Close to the bone on either side pressing at each acupressure point, all the way to the tailbone. "You can use oil to help if you want." I was correct. This was an anointed or blessed oil.

He continued to show me how to spread the energy on the back and then had Robert re-turn over. Ambrosio showed me how to massage the energy on the abdomen. He explained how, on most women, the abdomen needs to be massaged upward. Pulling the organs and the energy from either side of the pubic bone, up into the abdomen. "And you visualize the energy as well as the organs moving up."

"Now on men, you want to move the energy not so much up but more inwards towards the male parts."

He had me tune into Robert's whole body. I could actually see and feel where the energy was running and where it was stuck. Where there was less energy and where it was high. "Now feel where he needs more energy." Robert had two points on either side above his navel that appeared rosy pink. I mean in a psychic way not literally. I had the urge to spread the energy there.

"Yes, that's correct." Ambrosio noted as he watched me.

"Now if they have an issue with the heart, direct energy here." Ambrosio instructed placing his hands on Robert's heart. He moved his hands up and over placing his hands firmly over the left of his chest. "If they have a lung issue, put the energy here. The left side. This is the left lung. Now the right." He directed my hands on Robert's chest in the small muscular area under the shoulder. Just in front of either side of the armpits.

"Now spread the energy over the arms and legs."

My hands were on fire now and I could feel myself being spiritually guided, now one step ahead of my instruction.

"Now that's it. Pull it down the legs," Ambrosio said as I instinctively pulled the energy down.

I was now on an energetic high. Almost oblivious to my surroundings, working on automatic guidance, working in bliss.

"Now go into the sacral chakra," he instructed.

"You are doing wonderful. You are being guided." He encouraged me.

It was now time to open the body. I held my fingers like I

had seen Ambrosio. My index fingers and thumbs bend back out of the way and my other three fingers on each hand extended. I placed my middle fingers together just below Robert's navel. I breathed out hard pushing more energy into the area. My fingers were almost numb from the energy.

I was so out of it at this point. My eyes were half open, half closed and I was only partially in the room. One more push of energy and Ambrosio pulled my fingers and guided then apart. I didn't dare stare directly but out of my peripheral vision I saw a line of blood. I couldn't say if I felt my fingers inside his body. It was hard to tell. It was hard to tell anything physical at this point. It was as if they were no longer my fingers and I could no longer feel them. There was blood on Robert but had his body really opened? If so, I was sure it was Ambrosio's energy that had done this.

"Now close it with your hand," he said. I held both hands over the area and directed energy. When I dare look the skin was closed leaving just a little blood on the surface. Ambrosio quickly dabbed the area with cotton wool.

"Find the next point," Ambrosio said. I immediately found the center of his solar plexus chakra. Again Ambrosio guided my fingers as I breathed energy into the area. I felt at this point I might lose consciousness. I was so light headed, buzzing and high from the energy.

Ambrosio found the third point and I was just following on automatic pilot.

The psychic part was over and Ambrosio continued working on Robert's Kundalini. The rest was a blur. I made it through finishing up with Robert then I collapsed heavy on to the bed. I lay there like a log, my mind completely blank.

Ambrosio came to me. Yes I needed some of that revival energy he had given me the days before. He felt my forehead and my hands.

"You're extremely hot. Do you have a fever?" he said, highly concerned. I couldn't answer. Nicole confirmed that I was "very hot." Later I reminded him that my hands were freezing cold at the start. And no, I didn't have a fever! No, I wasn't sick or something. I just felt like I had been plugged into high voltage box and left there until my head almost exploded. That's why I was hot!

They stepped out on the patio just for a little break and left me there, lying on the bed for a while. When they returned, it was my turn for my third healing. I was not yet back in this world but I supposed it don't matter I was going to be lying and receiving now anyway.

I was pretty out of it all through this healing. It felt beautiful as it had previously. I also had the eye treatment, at least this time, I kinda knew what to expect.

I don't remember much else just that I passed out.

Ambrosio must have left. I still lay in the bed exactly as I had been after the session. Robert was knocked out too. The two of us were hopeless. We couldn't stand up after one of these treatments. Having done one myself the energy was even greater. I remained in the same position I had dropped and didn't move an inch. We both slept for hours.

At just before sunset I was able to drag myself out and meditate. I wanted to do it while I was still in this energy veil. I sent a message on Facebook and Twitter that I was doing this. I hoped that everyone back home could feel just a little bit of what I was feeling and receive this amazing energy.

Robert and I had just enough energy to stagger to the restaurant next door for a quick bite. We recapped what had happened.

"You think receiving a session makes you feel like you've been hit over the head with a sledge hammer and have a swarm of locusts in your head. That is nothing compared to giving this type of healing!" I told Robert.

"How am I going to be able to do this? I'm just assisting him and I can't stand up. One session on someone and I'll have to rest for 24 hours!" I was realizing that there is such a tremendous surge of energy required to do this work.

"Did you really feel like your body was opened?" I asked him. He wasn't completely sure. If it had actually happened I was convinced it was all Ambrosio's doing.

Tomorrow I was going to be in charge of giving Robert a healing and we would see. He was going to be my first official volunteer to practice on tomorrow.

"…and, by the way, that means you're getting your eyeball licked tomorrow."

"Yuck." Robert would do pretty much anything for me but this…? He was not looking forward to having his eyeball licked!

Then by 7 p.m. it was bedtime and we were out again.

I vaguely remember waking a little afterwards and deciding to continue my story on my computer. I was strangely surprised to see the amount I had written. I didn't remember writing all this. Then I read details that I had written the night before that included things that just happened today. How was that possible? Had I written these notes today? No I hadn't been on my computer. I appeared to have written almost an entire book. And some of the details I had written, I was sure I had written before they even happened. What was going on here? Was I imagining this? Or was this a strange form of Déjà vu?

CHAPTER 13

Opening of the Chakras

Today was my big day. Ambrosio was going to open my chakras and give me the official initiation, the passing of "The Gift." I knew from what Robert told me, blood might appear on my chakras. I must admit I was a bit nervous. I took the time to meditate and balance myself and asked for any fear to be taken away. I asked to be worthy of receiving this gift.

Ambrosio and Nicole arrived earlier today. It was a big day for all of us. He took me aside to talk outside for a while away from the camera. He wanted to have a serious conversation with me. "Today will be a big change for you. Are you sure you really want this?" he asked.

I was very sure.

He told me his plans were not to do psychic surgery here anymore. Not to go to Russia anymore but just to help me and assist me if I needed it. We had talked about a trip to America and he agreed it would be good. But he was thinking of that as a trip to continue training me. He thought it would be good for me to return to Baguio and possibly bring clients. But his focus now would be to continue helping me until such time I didn't need him. I told him that he didn't need to give up his work for me and he could certainly still go to Russia if he wanted to.

"No. It's time," he said, simply and gently.

His words lingered in the air and we both cried and hugged.

"Besides, I am going to return to the provinces where I'm from so I can see my little girl grow up," he added, trying to cheer both of us up.

"Ok, then. We have a big day, Gail."

First the opening of the chakras and the initiation. I was glad he had me lie down because, of course, as soon as he started the prayers the veil came over me. If I had any fear it was now replaced with pure love. I had my eyes closed and I was in a world of my own, so most of it I don't remember, I just had the video to review later.

Much of the prayers and initiation was in Tagalog. It sounded beautiful and sacred but the words just drifted around me. I heard him ask that the power and the energy be given to me. I saw what I believe must have been his mother, perhaps his grandmother smiling at the end of the bed. This vision must have been in my mind's eye, as I still had my eyes closed.

I felt him working on each chakra in a similar way to the psychic surgery. It was especially powerful in my palms. My fingertips were buzzing with energy and I could feel the clockwise rotation of the energy in my palms. I have noticed that my energy at rest, rotates counterclockwise and gently in my palms. Now it was clockwise and spinning wildly. It was a pure white energy with a glow of pink. In the video you saw a drop of blood in the center of each palm appear.

As he worked on my third eye a kaleidoscope of colors opened up with mostly purple and blue tones. As it settled I could see the room and everyone in it even though I had my eyes closed! I could see but this time it was in two tone. A kind of dark bluish purple. *Oh, this is what it looks like through my third eye.* I looked around the room and could see in every direction all whist my eyes remained closed.

I believe he opened up my Kundalini, working on each point down my spine. It felt like little pockets of energy popped at each vertebrae. To be honest at this point I was floating above my body in complete bliss.

He finished. It took me a moment to get back into my own body and come back to earth. I felt markedly different. Though I am not sure I can explain how. A very solid, grounded feeling, yet a feeling of being also highly connected to the other side.

It was a huge influx of energy and I was also very emotional. I hugged Ambrosio and he hugged me back. He smiled in acknowledgement that I had been given "The Gift." I had been given his energy.

I felt very different, though I am not sure I can explain how. I had to sit for a moment to completely take this in. It was time to perform my first psychic surgery and Nicole was my volunteer. I needed to rest a little and drink water before I could even stand to now perform a healing.

This time I was to do a session on my own, with Ambrosio guiding me, of course. "I am now your assistant," he said. I was still on cloud nine and the energy was extremely strong. I now stood on the healer side of the massage table, Ambrosio on the assistant side. I said the prayers and called in my loved ones and my guides. I felt the little Filipino lady, Ester with me. I asked to connect to Divine and to be a channel for the healing. Ambrosio looked on as my guide and assistant. I felt the energy rise in a sudden surge and the spirits very close to me. This gave me a confidence that maybe I could do this.

I started with the Magnetic Healing. First tuning in. Then holding my hands over Nicole's chakras. Ambrosio looked on and didn't intervene, just nodded quietly in encouragement. I placed my hands over her heart. I placed my left hand. Then on top of my left hand, I placed my right hand. I breathed the energy into her heart and I felt the energy start to spin. Then I saw a third hand over mine. A small hand, made from light. A spirit hand. I knew this magnetic healing was the real healing taking place. As this third hand came over the energy raised several times more.

I worked on the other chakras, each time I placed my left hand, then my right, then a third light-being hand appeared. I breathed the energy down through me and into her chakra. I turned her over and worked on her Kundalini down either side of the spine. The intention was to release the energy at each point down the spine. I felt the energy release like popping a bubble of light. I turned her back. I empowered the chakras, felt them spinning and then spread this energy. The vibration in my body went higher and higher. My palms were pulsating. I heard the thousand locusts clearly that Robert had been talking about the whole time. I was half here, half not here. Floating and working from instinct.

With my eyes half open and breathing the energy, I placed my fingers in position for psychic surgery. My two middle fingers together, I breathed the energy through them and into her body.

I visualized penetrating her soul body. This took a tremendous amount of energy and I felt extremely light headed. I was ready to do psychic surgery. Still I wasn't convinced I could do this on my own. I believe there was a moment of hesitation and I looked at Ambrosio as if to say "Ok, I think I need help with this part."

Nothing was said, but Ambrosio leaned in and held my fingers, gently guiding them apart. I squeezed the energy through and into the body as I did and my eyes rolled back and half closed. From my peripheral vision I saw a line appear across her abdomen. I was not able to look straight on or think clearly as I did this. I wanted to. I wanted to be present and really see what was happening, yet for it to happen I had to be on this tremendous spiritual high where I could not concentrate no matter how hard I tried. I felt that if I looked too directly it would not work. I had to somehow take my concentration out of what was happening on a physical level and just let it be. I needed to concentrate the energy on a spiritual level. I felt if there was a moment of hesitation or mistrust it would not happen. I felt even concentrating on it in a physical way or putting attention on it would somehow prevent the very thing from happening that I was concentrating on. Just like when you try to be clairvoyant and see things, the more you try, the less it works. I believed great faith and energy must be put in this but not energy in a way one would normally concentrate, rather the complete opposite.

I continued the session, only half there, only half conscious. Ambrosio held my fingers and assisted me. Yes the skin appeared to part and blood pooled around my fingers. Still I was not convinced it was my doing.

Then for a moment, I was not in my body, I was up in the

air slightly back from the table. I was looking at me performing the surgery. I was watching the entire scene unfold but this time I was watching from outside of my body. I was looking at me doing the surgery. At this point I was no longer feeling and performing as Gail. I was looking in from an independent view. I was behind Ambrosio at the opposite side of the massage table looking back at myself. I appeared to be working away in a very confident manner.

Then I noticed the side of my face. I saw the birth mark. What?! That was impossible! It was not me! It was Ambrosio! I was Ambrosio! Yet in my vision I was floating just above and behind Ambrosio. In fact, I could see Ambrosio standing just in front of me. Even though his back was turned to me it looked like him and I could see him still moving about. I was also looking straight at me at the other side of the table performing the surgery. But the "me" I saw, was also Ambrosio. I thought it was me. Yet, I recognized him from the birth mark or was I recognizing me?

The vision faded and without notice I was back in the scene performing "surgery." I did not seem to be thrown by this vision at all but continued on, doing the healing on Nicole.

It was only later that I thought about this out of body experience and questioned it. Had I imagined this? Had I imagined the vision? Had I imagined I was doing psychic surgery. Was I really doing it? Or was it Ambrosio? Or was it all just an illusion? Why was I shown the birthmark if it was really me? And was it really me?

CHAPTER 14

It All Comes Together

I didn't share this vision with Ambrosio. I suppose a part of me thought that he knew. That he was somehow a part of this and had experienced it with me. It was as if in this moment of heightened state we were working as one, so everything I knew, he knew also. Perhaps that was why I saw myself both as me and him at the same time. Perhaps we were both one at the same time. Still I knew I didn't need to share verbally. I knew we both already knew.

I was confident there would be a long and deep connection between us, no matter where we both were in the world. I knew that he would now be with me as a healer, whether he would be physically present or not.

As we finished up, Ambrosio smiled at me. "You are getting it very fast." He said, "You are now ready."

Ready? On one level I was anything but ready. I was not in the least sure I could do any of this without him standing next to me. Yet on another level, I knew he would be standing next to me.

As the session ended, I was very overwhelmed by the energy. Once again I had to lie down. As Ambrosio worked on me he encouraged me not to worry.

"You will get used to this energy and you will be fine."

I looked less than confident.

"You will see. Your clients will tell you how they feel. Your clients will show you how they are healed and this will be your confirmation. As healers we are always the ones that question our work. You will be the only enemy. You will be the one that lacks the faith. But you will see from your clients. It is them that will show you that what you do is very powerful."

He laughed as he hugged me, knowing I was having a hard time trusting.

"And don't worry, I will be there as your assistant for as long as you need me."

I told him, I could see myself using this gift in the magnetic healing and bringing it into my work in many ways. But as far as the actual physical surgery, I could not imagine doing it without him there.

"You will see," he said.

"And remember the magnetic healing is the real healing".

We hugged and said goodbye, knowing that we were not parting at all. This was only the beginning of our partnership in healing.

On the bus ride back, I mused about what I had learned. I thought about the whole experience. The healing. Did it really happen? Was all of it real or just some of it? Where was it going to go from here? Finally, after many hours, my mind switched off, and I watched the fields pass by. I was lulled into that half-awake, half-asleep state.

I found myself back in the past life vision that I had experienced before, back in this ancient time, long ago. As the "doctor" stood in front of me, we both knew his predicament. You see, his healing gift was prescient of the gods. For it was believed that the healer in the village was given a gift, bestowed by the gods, and that the god of healing was truly the one who actually cured the people. The fact that the doctor had apparently lost his gift, meant that he must have wronged or upset the gods in some way. If the people in the village were dying, it was a sure sign the doctor was deemed cursed by the gods. Nothing could return favor to the village, except to sacrifice the life of the doctor. I was helpless to intervene, as in doing so I would also have been going against the will of the gods.

The people were angry and afraid. They were calling for this "offering" to the gods, lest they remain cursed. It was life or death for them. Either the gods needed to be appeased or they could lose another child from the plague. His bloodshed was needed for the faith of the people to return. There was little I could do. If I had spoken out, not only would it have been useless, but I would have been seen as a defender of this ungodly curse.

His eyes locked mine and we had a telepathic communication. I asked for forgiveness. He knew his fate and was resigned to it. "Don't worry the healing gift will continue and peace will return," he told me silently. He was carried off to sacrifice his life. I felt helpless and I knew on some level that these healing gods could not be so cruel. Yet I could do nothing about it. His life was taken by a stake to the side of his head, just in front of the left ear.

I couldn't bear to be there, yet I knew the moment it

happened. I knew from that very moment, he was around me. He was always with me and his gift was now within me. I wouldn't perform healing, yet I knew just being among the people, I was able to bring calm and healing to the village. Even though he was no longer in physical form he continued his healing mission on the other side.

A sense of peace and tranquility came over me as the vision slowly faded and I gradually became awake. I looked out at the fields passing by with a renewed feeling of serenity. They were *perfectly, perfect*, I thought. Everything was as it should be.

This book was written in the three nights I was in Baguio. How is this possible? I don't know. But then, anything is possible on the spiritual realms.

Acknowledgments

With deep appreciation, I thank the following people:

Most importantly, my family: my Mom and my girls, who believe in me and support me through my crazy adventures. For it would not be possible for me to either write or do my work without their beautiful and loving acceptance.

Of course, to Robert Pellegrino-Estrich for setting me on this exciting journey, for holding the camera, and for generally putting up with me.

For those who made this particular journey wonderful; Ketut, Cakoda, Nicole and Marti in Bali and Anthony Vivero, Nicole and Emmi in the Philippines.

A special thank you to my Auntie Pauline, my Reiki teacher, and her son, my cousin Ric, my spiritual sounding boards. And my mentor, John of God for the connection and inspiration.

Great photo contributions from Kevin Ellsworth, as well as others. To Dawn from Teagarden Designs for the cover and layout.

To those who created a forum for me, particularly Robert of

the Conscious Life Expo, Ken of the New Living Expo, Mark of the New Life Expo, Steve and Megan of Body Mind Spirit Expo, Chandler of Body Soul Spirit, Anne of Mind Body Spirit and Patricia and Jacquie at Conscious Living Australia. Dannion who was saved by the light, and Peter for guiding me. TJ for getting the word out and Digby from Avalon for my spiritual bling.

And those dear friends who work tirelessly so I can do this work: Cindy N, Rory, Cindy R, Michelle, Sami, Leah and many more.

A special mention to my dear friend Mark, who has supported me from the beginning of my journey.

To Dr. Dave for taking care of me, believing in me and just for being there.

And especially to my spiritual group and friends who have attended, volunteered, and supported me at my events.

But most of all, my deep gratitude to Ambrosio for your generous devotion to healing in this lifetime and others.

And to God, for through God, all things are possible....

About the Author

Gail Thackray was raised in Yorkshire, England and prides herself on having kept her British down-to-earth sensibility. Her life changed at age forty when she discovered she was a medium and able to talk to spirits on the other side. Opening up to the spirit world, she realized she was also able to channel healing energy, manifest more easily, and even talk to animals. Helping others connect to Source and to develop their own natural psychic abilities is her passion.

Gail loves to travel and is the star of a series *Gail Thackray's Spiritual Journeys* where she brings us extraordinary people and places around the world. You can join Gail on one of her spiritual adventures. She regularly takes clients to John of God, the spiritual healer in Brazil, and now plans to take clients to the Philippines. Gail lectures at events worldwide, doing live appearances as a healer and medium. When at home in Los Angeles, she writes, lectures, and teaches about mediumship, healing, animal communication, manifesting, and other aspects of spirituality.

If you are interested in a trip to the Philippines to meet the psychic surgeons or want to participate in Gail's other retreats or spiritual journeys, please visit her website:

www.GailThackray.com

www.ingramcontent.com/pod-product-compliance
Lightning Source LLC
Chambersburg PA
CBHW051814040426
42446CB00007B/666

* 9 7 8 0 9 8 6 1 3 3 8 1 7 *